African Textualities

Texts, Pre-Texts and Contexts of African Literature

Bernth Lindfors

Africa World Press, Inc.

P.O. Box 1892
Trenton, NJ 08607

P.O. Box 48
Asmara, ERITREA

Africa World Press, Inc.

P.O. Box 1892
Trenton, NJ 08607

P.O. Box 48
Asmara, ERITREA

Cover Design: Linda Nickens

Library of Congress Cataloging-in-Publication Data

Lindfors, Bernth.
    African textualities : texts, pretexts, and contexts of African literature / Bernth Lindfors.
        p. cm.
    Includes bibliographical references. (p.   ) and index.
    ISBN 0-86543-615-0 (cloth). -- ISBN 0-86543-616-9 (paper)
    1. African literature--History and criticism.   2. Canon (Literature) I. Title.
PL8010.L5   1997
809' .8896--dc21   97-4356
                                                                  CIP

Table of Contents

African Textualities

Table of Contents, continued

Acknowledgements

I am grateful to the editors of *Africa Today, African Literature Association Bulletin, America, Ba Shiru, Bayreuth African Studies Series, Colby Library Quarterly, Commonwealth: Essays and Studies, A Current Bibliography on African Affairs, English in Africa,* and *International Fiction Review* as well as to the book editors of *A Talent(ed) Digger: Creations, Cameos and Essays in Honour of Anna Rutherford* and the Collier-Macmillan edition of *Mission to Kala* for permission to reprint material that first appeared in their pages. Every effort has been made to trace the owners of copyright to all lengthy quotations, but in a few cases this has proved impossible; I would like to hear from any who have been missed.

I also wish to express my gratitude to Douglas Brown, archivist at Groton School, for supplying me with photocopies of school publications and documents and for granting me permission to quote from them, and I want to thank Alan Pifer and Adrian Sherwood for allowing me to quote from their letters about Ayi Kwei Armah. Photos of Armah have been reproduced from Armah's application for admission to Groton School, from the 1960 Groton School Yearbook and from Harvard University's freshman *Register* for the Class of 1964. The photos and cartoons of Chinua Achebe have been reproduced from *Government College,Umuahia Magazine*, from the *Guardian* (Lagos), from the *New York Review of Books*, and from Achebe's personal files. I am very grateful for permission to use these interesting visuals.

I also wish to thank Malcolm Hacksley and his staff at the National English Literary Museum in Grahamstown for providing me with numerous photocopies from their newspaper cuttings files on *Sarafina 2* and Mbongeni Ngema. The cartoons on *Sarafina 2* have been reprinted from S. Francis, H. Dugmore and Rico's *Madam and Eve: Somewhere Over the Rainbow* (Parktown:

Penguin Books South Africa, 1996). Permission to use them is gratefully acknowledged.

Finally, a special word of thanks to Cinde Hastings for quickly and efficiently preparing the final camera-ready copy for this book.

Introduction

African literary texts can be approached in a variety of ways. They may be examined in isolation as verbal artefacts that have a unique integrity. They may be studied in relation to other texts that preceded and followed them. Or they may be seen against the backdrop of the times, traditions and circumstances that helped to shape them. In this book all these approaches have been utilized, sometimes singly, sometimes in combination.

The section on Texts opens by briefly surveying the career of Chinua Achebe as a novelist and then focuses on four texts, two by famous West African authors (Achebe and Beti) and two by unknown South African writers (Singh and Bruin), one of whom is presented in disguise. Here the method is descriptive and analytical rather than contextual or theoretical.

In Pre-Texts the emphasis is on what preceded the major works of Ayi Kwei Armah, Amos Tutuola and Chinua Achebe. Two chapters deal with the essays and short stories Armah composed at Groton School and Harvard University before he returned to Ghana and started writing novels. Another attempts to assess the extent of Tutuola's debt to oral storytelling by identifying motifs in *The Palm-Wine Drinkard* that can be found in West African folktales. And a short note illustrated with photographs and caricatures of Achebe shows how he looked to the camera and to the cartoonist at various points in his career. All these 'pre-texts" are extra-textual in the sense that they concentrate on matters external to or antedating the fictions that made these authors famous. They are background studies.

The section on Contexts, on the other hand, tends to be concerned with larger diachronic issues. The first essay interrogates the concept of national literatures in Africa. The next two seek to trace changing patterns in the development of modern African literatures in colonial and postcolonial times. Then surprising transformations in the careers of Peter Abrahams and Mbongeni Ngema are discussed, and the section concludes with a tribute to Ken Saro-Wiwa, the Nigerian author recently executed by the Abacha regime. Each essay thus documents twists and turns in the making of Africa's literary history.

Texts

Achebe's Escort Service

In Chinua Achebe's fifth novel *Anthills of the Savannah* (1987) a wise old man insists that storytelling is more important to a community than drumming or fighting a war:

> Why? Because it is only the story can continue beyond the war and the warrior. It is the story that outlives the sound of war-drums and the exploits of brave fighters. It is the story, not the others, that saves our progeny from blundering like blind beggars into the spikes of the cactus fence. The story is our escort; without it, we are blind. Does the blind man own his escort? No, neither do we the story; rather it is the story that owns us and directs us. (124)

Over the last century Africa has experienced a great deal of turmoil, has heard many war-drums and seen lots of battles. Initially these were colonial conflicts; today they tend to be civil wars or struggles between unelected leaders and the peoples they misrule. The story of these turbulent years has not been an easy one to tell, but many writers have taken a stab at it, putting on record at least a small portion of Africa's contemporary history in instructive fictional terms.

Of these storytellers no one has been more successful than Chinua Achebe. His novels have offered us not just lucid instruction but also profound enlightenment, enabling us to see more clearly what has happened in Africa and why. His stories have been our escort, our most reliable guide to that continent's troubled past and troubling present. He has made it impossible for us to remain blind to African realities.

Achebe's first novel *Things Fall Apart* (1958) was set in a traditional Ibo village community in eastern Nigeria at the turn of the century when the first missionaries and colonial administrative officials were beginning to penetrate inland. Its hero was Okonkwo, a famous warrior and expert farmer who had risen to become a wealthy and respected leader of his clan. Achebe's rich portrayal of traditional Ibo society glowed with compassion. The customs, rituals, beliefs and institutions that regulated the lives of villagers before the arrival of the white man were sympathetically depicted and shown to be worthy of our respect. Okonkwo and his people were obviously not living in a state of wild savagery and barbarism. Theirs was a well-ordered society perfectly adapted to its environment.

But at the same time Achebe made no attempt to conceal some bad features of traditional Ibo life, including wife beating, caste taboos, and infanticide. He also recognized that among Ibo men a very heavy emphasis was placed on proving oneself a man by displays of extraordinary strength or courage; this was partly what ultimately brought Okonkwo down when he tried single-handedly to halt the encroachments Europe had made on his community. In order to help us understand the full dimensions of Okonkwo's tragedy, Achebe tried to present a balanced view of Ibo society that took into account its internal weaknesses as well as its strengths.

When the two cultures eventually collided, the weaker one gave way. Achebe was careful to show that the collapse of traditional African society was due as much to internal infirmity as to external force, that the society unwilling to bend must eventually break. But he also demonstrated quite convincingly that this particular African society would have been able to survive quite a long time had it not been for Europe's sudden intrusion into its midst. His novel revealed that Ibo villages were well-organized and democratically governed, that there were religious and legal constraints on an individual's behavior, and that achievement was prized, making it possible for a hard-working man to rise to a high position in the clan regardless of his parentage. Ibo society, to put it briefly, was civilized and stable, not primitive and chaotic. Then, with the coming of the white man, things fell apart and anarchy was loosed upon the Ibo world. The white men, in other words, were not bringers of light to a dark continent, as was popularly supposed, and their "civilizing mission" did not result in peace, order and harmony. Rather, they were ignorant servants of a powerful queen who disrupted a well-ordered, cohesive, pacific society by imposing on it their own forms of government and religious worship. Achebe thus reinterpreted African history, seeing it through African eyes.

His interpretation was objective, honest and fair to all sides. Although his sympathies were primarily with the Ibo villagers, he understood the colonial mentality of his European characters well enough to portray them not as black-hearted villains or monsters but as convincing human beings whose actions were motivated by dedication to an ideal. His purpose was to examine Africa's first confrontation with Europe from an African point of view, yet he managed to stand sufficiently aloof from the encounter so that his vision was not blurred by emotion. He saw and made us see the misunderstandings that precipitated conflict, the chain of events that inevitably led to tragedy. And because he never lost sight of the larger dimensions of his story, specific actions always took on a wider significance that gave them paradigmatic value. Achebe evidently was talking not just about Okonkwo and Iboland but also about other Africans elsewhere and indeed about all colonized people wherever they happened to be.

This novel, which has sold in the millions to readers all over the world, has probably done more to reshape the image of Africa in colonial times than any other single book. It enabled everyone—Africans as well as non-Africans—to view African experience from an indigenous perspective, and it did this in a wholly satisfactory artistic manner, persuading us as much by its aesthetic elegance as by its powerful argument. It was Africa's first modern classic.

Part of what distinguished this novel was the limpid and versatile style in which it was written. Instead of having his British and Ibo characters speak in the same idiom, Achebe devised for his kinsmen an African vernacular style that simulated expression in their native tongue. Ibo words, figures of speech and proverbs were translated virtually verbatim and introduced into appropriate passages of dialogue and exposition. These expressions were inserted so skillfully that they served not as exotic verbal ornaments but as functional agents of characterization and cultural description. Achebe thus succeeded in giving the English language a new prose style, an African style that perfectly suited his African message.

His next novel, *No Longer at Ease* (1960), intended as a sequel to *Things Fall Apart*, was set in the capital of Nigeria in the late 1950s and had as its hero Okonkwo's grandson, Obi Okonkwo, a young, Westernized bureaucrat who finds himself torn between two cultures—the old and the new. Although he comes back from his university studies in England with high ideals and a determination to prove himself an honest, hard-working civil servant, he eventually slides into corruption because he is unable to reconcile the demands placed upon him by his Westernized girlfriend and by his tradition-bound parents. Like his grandfather, Obi was another victim of culture conflict, the major difference being that now the conflict was psychological rather than physical. Obi had been weaned away from traditional values, but he had not fully assimilated Western ideals, so having no firm moral convictions, he was confused by his predicament and fell.

But again, as in *Things Fall Apart* Achebe did not try to blame his fall entirely on Europe. He acknowledged the weaknesses within traditional society as well as the human frailty of his hero. His intention was simply to show us what his people had lost during the colonial encounter, and he felt that one of their greatest misfortunes was their forfeiture of a clear code of moral values. It is this spiritual loss that left Obi and his society no longer at ease in the modern world.

In his next novel, *Arrow of God* (1964), Achebe turned back to the 1920s to fill in the temporal gap between his first two works. This time he chose as his hero a headstrong Chief Priest of an Ibo snake cult who fell victim to the changing times and to his own towering pride. Ezeulu attempted to come to terms with the innovations introduced into his world by the church and the colonial administration, and this angered some of his followers and rivals. In the end he was destroyed by his compromise with Europe, for this undermined his position in the community. When Europe later betrayed him, he chose to take a foolishly proud stand in an effort to reestablish his authority, but he had already lost too much ground with his people so he quickly fell, descending finally into isolation and madness.

Arrow of God was Achebe's longest, most complex and most successful novel, possessing a richness of texture, depth of characterization, and ambiguity that cannot be found in his other fiction. The ambiguity derived from Achebe's enigmatical depiction of Ezeulu. Was the priest merely an "arrow in the bow of his god," was he the victim of *hubris*, or was he mad? The novel provided no clear answer to this question, leaving readers to ponder the nature of the perplexing relationship between a priest and his god.

The religious drama in *Arrow of God* was played out against the backdrop of the colonial drama in Nigeria. Achebe was actually telling two stories at once, interweaving them with such skill that they could not be separated. Ezeulu, a guardian of the old order, must be destroyed before the new order can firmly establish itself in Iboland. Missionaries and European administrative officials subvert the old priest's authority in the clan and thereby precipitate his fall. The forces of change, which Ezeulu had hoped to forestall, thus overwhelm him and transform his society. The battle of cultures is once again won by Europe.

In his fourth novel, *A Man of the People* (1966), Achebe brought the historical record right up to contemporary times. Indeed, this novel, published only nine days after Nigeria experienced its first military coup, even ended with a military coup. It appeared that Achebe had predicted with uncanny accuracy the end of his country's first republic.

But the novel no doubt was intended as a political parable, not as a prophecy. It had as its central character a corrupt politician who had elbowed his way into prominence and power. But M.A. Nanga, one of the finest rogues in African fiction, was only a symptom of a sick postcolonial African society; one needed to look into the very heart of the body politic to account for such a diseased member. Achebe's diagnosis was that people who had recently passed through a period of colonial rule adopted a rather cynical attitude toward political corruption. They were willing to excuse the extravagances of their leaders because they believed that these men who had led the struggle for political independence now had a right to eat "the national cake." They also believed that a well-fed M.P. might let a few crumbs fall to his constituents. Such cynicism kept hungry men like Nanga in power and perpetuated a tradition of corruption in government. The sick society had to undergo a major political convulsion before such cynicism was transmuted into hope.

Although *A Man of the People* was a comedy and ended happily with Nanga's removal from government, it remained, like Achebe's other novels, a disturbingly pessimistic work. While censuring Africa for allowing itself to be corrupted by forces from within and without, Achebe again indicted Europe for contributing to the moral confusion and political chaos that beset independent African states. His characters were representative men and women of their time yet emblematic of the ills and malaise that afflicted modern African society. Nothing seemed completely right in so debauched a world.

In Nigeria that confusion and chaos were to lead first to military rule and then to full-fledged civil war. During this period Achebe stopped writing novels altogether, but in the aftermath of the war he turned his hand to poetry, short fiction, essays and speech-writing. It was not until 1987, a full twenty-one years after *A Man of the People*, that he published another novel, *Anthills of the Savannah*. In this new work he picked up more or less where he had left off, focusing a sharp eye on the military elite that had ruled Nigeria and many other African countries after the collapse of democratically elected regimes.

The focal character, a Sandhurst graduate who has risen to the top position in his nation after a military coup and who clearly relishes being called "Your Excellency," wishes to be proclaimed President-for-Life. When his ambitions are frustrated, he feels insecure and angry and seeks to punish those he perceives as his foes, including two of his closest school buddies. In the end all three men are killed, and their friends, associates and lovers are left to pick up the pieces. There is a suggestion that out of this newfound unity among the long-suffering masses in Africa something positive will emerge, but one of the central questions raised in the course of the narrative—"What must a people do to appease an embittered history?"—remains unanswered. Perhaps things have fallen so far apart in modern Africa there is little that can be done by the powerless except to form alliances among themselves and hope that one day their suffering will end. But their future does not look particularly bright.

Throughout his career Achebe has kept pace with the times by responding to the changing preoccupations of his society. Forty years ago he was a reconstructionist dedicated to creating a dignified image of the African past; today he is an angry reformer crusading against the immorality and injustices of the African present. His novels thus not only chronicle one hundred years of Nigerian history but also reflect the dominant African intellectual concerns of the past four decades.

For this reason one suspects his novels will have enduring significance. Later generations of readers will find in them an interpretation of African experience that is characteristic of its time. The compassionate evocations of Ibo village life, the graphic depictions of modern city life, the brilliantly drawn characters will probably speak with as much power then as they do today, eloquently recalling crucial moments in that confused era in Nigeria's past which began with the arrival of the first white men and ended with the imposition and perpetuation of indigenous military rule. Tomorrow as well as today Achebe's novels will remain our trusty escorts, guiding us to a better understanding of an eventful century in African history.

Ambiguity and Intention in
Arrow of God

To understand Chinua Achebe's *Arrow of God* one must comprehend Ezeulu's deep concern over the way his world is changing. This concern is expressed both in his decision to send one of his sons to a mission school and in the arguments he uses to justify his decision. He tells his son that a man must move with the times: "I am like the bird Eneke-nti-oba. When his friends asked him why he was always on the wing he replied: 'Men of today have learnt to shoot without missing and so I have learnt to fly without perching.'...The world is like a Mask dancing. If you want to see it well you do not stand in one place" (55). Months later Ezeulu reminds his son that he must learn the white man's magic because "a man must dance the dance prevalent in his time" (234). Ezeulu explains his decision to the village elders by comparing the white man to a new disease:

> A disease that has never been seen before cannot be cured with everyday herbs. When we want to make a charm we look for the animal whose blood can match its power; if a chicken cannot do it we look for a goat or a ram; if that is not sufficient we send for a bull. But sometimes even a bull does not suffice, then we must look for a human. (165)

Ezulu's son is to be the human sacrifice that will enable the clan to make medicine of sufficient strength to hold the new disease in check. In other words, Ezeulu decides to sacrifice his son in order to gain power to cope with the changing times.

It is this willingness to attempt to come to terms with change that differentiates Ezeulu from Okonkwo, the hero of *Things Fall Apart*. Achebe himself has said:

> Ezeulu, the chief character in *Arrow of God*, is a different kind of man from Okonkwo. He is an intellectual. He thinks about why things happen—he is a priest and his office requires this—so he goes into the roots of things and he's ready to accept change, intellectually. He sees the value of change and therefore his reaction to Europe is completely different from Okonkwo's. He is ready to come to terms with it—up to a point—except where his dignity is involved. This he could not accept; he is very proud. So you see it's really the other side of the coin, and the tragedy is that they come to the same sticky end. So there's really no escape whether you accept change or whether you don't. (Serumaga iii-iv)

Okonkwo and Ezeulu are two early casualties in the war of cultures in Africa. Okonkwo dies because he refuses to surrender. Ezeulu is destroyed because he compromises with Europe and in so doing allows alien forces to undermine his position; when Europe later betrays him, he takes a foolishly proud stand in an effort to reestablish his authority, but he has already lost too much ground with his people and quickly falls.

The attitude of his people towards the white man is almost entirely negative. They say, "As daylight chases away darkness so will the white man drive away all our customs...he has come to make trouble for us" (105-06). They are therefore very unhappy with Ezeulu's decision to send his son Oduche to the mission school, regarding the deed as an irresponsible gesture of friendship toward their enemy. Ezeulu, they feel, should have acted with more circumspection and foresight, should have led the struggle against the alien religion instead of exposing his own child to its abhorrent teachings. Thus, when Captain Winterbottom, the white District Officer, curtly commands Ezeulu to appear in his office within twenty-four hours and Ezeulu calls the elders together to ask if they think he should heed the summons, one unfriendly elder replies in no uncertain terms that Ezeulu must either suffer the consequences of friendship with the white man or do something to end the friendship.

> Or does Ezeulu think that their friendship should stop short of entering each other's houses? Does he want the white man to be his friend only by word of mouth? Did not our elders tell us that as soon as we shake hands with a leper he will want an embrace?...What I say is this...a man who brings ant-ridden faggots into his hut should expect the visit of lizards. But if Ezeulu is now telling us that he is tired of the white man's friendship our advice to him should be: You tied the knot, you should also know how to undo it. You passed the shit that is smelling; you should carry it away. Fortunately the evil charm brought in at the end of a pole is not too difficult to take outside again. (177-78)

Ezeulu does not take kindly to criticism from his peers, usually choosing either to ignore it or to act in deliberate defiance of it. He is particularly sensitive on the matter of Oduche's education and refuses to allow anyone to question his decision. When a close friend accuses him of betraying his people by allying himself with the white man, Ezeulu counters, pointing out that he did not bring the white man to his people; rather his people brought the white man upon themselves by failing to oppose him when he first arrived. If they wish to blame someone, they should blame themselves for meekly submitting to the white man's presence and power. Ezeulu then quotes the same proverb that the other employs against him. "The man who brings ant-infested faggots into his hut should not grumble when lizards begin to pay him a visit" (163). This is a key proverb in *Arrow of God*. It enunciates a major theme: that a man is responsible for his actions and must bear their consequences.

But Ezeulu is not an ordinary man. Because he is the priest of Ulu he can claim that his actions are sanctioned or prompted by his god. And this is indeed how Ezeulu explains much of his behavior. When he opposes his clan's decision to wage war against a neighboring clan, when he testifies against his own people in a legal dispute over the ownership of certain lands, when he refuses to perform the seasonal ritual that permits new yams to be harvested, he invariably announces that he is acting on behalf of Ulu, his deity. After such an announcement he is absolutely inflexible; no one can change his opinion or alter his stance, though elders may, and often do, question the truth of his assertion. The real question is whether Ezeulu the man or Ulu the god should be held responsible for the priest's actions.

The worst crisis brought on by Ezeulu's religiously inspired intransigence is the yam-harvesting crisis. Elders of the clan plead with him, coax him, then command him to do his priestly duty by performing the necessary ritual. When they remind him of his responsibility to his people, Ezeulu answers that he has a higher responsibility to his god. The elders then offer to accept all blame for the performance of the ritual, but Ezeulu answers, "you cannot say: do what is not done and we shall take the blame. I am the Chief Priest of Ulu and what I have told you is his will not mine" (260-61). Ezeulu sincerely believes that he is the instrument of a divine power, "an arrow in the bow of his god" (241). When his actions bring disaster upon himself and his people, he does not feel responsible but rather feels betrayed by his god:

> Why, he asked himself again and again, why had Ulu chosen to deal thus with him, to strike him down and cover him with mud? What was his offence? Had he not divined the god's will and obeyed it? When was it ever heard that a child was scalded by the piece of yam its own mother put in its palm? What man would send his son with a potsherd to bring fire from a neighbour's hut and then unleash rain on him? Who ever sent his son up the palm to gather nuts and then took an axe and felled the tree? (286)

Tortured by these questions, Ezeulu finally goes mad. His people turn away from him and Ulu and begin worshipping the white man's god.

Ezeulu's downfall thus marks the end of an era of unflinching allegiance to tribal gods and traditional ways. After Ezeulu ruins himself and his priesthood, his people are more receptive to new religious ideas and unfamiliar Western institutions such as schools, churches, and administrative offices. They are on the road to detribalization. Achebe once again succeeds in giving his hero's personal tragedy a wider dimension of significance.

Arrow of God is Achebe's longest, most complex, and most successful novel. It possesses a richness of texture, depth of characterization, and ambiguity that cannot be found in his other fiction. The ambiguity derives from Achebe's enigmatical depiction of Ezeulu. Is the priest merely an "arrow in the bow of his god," is he the victim of *hubris*, or is he mad? The novel provides no clear answer to this question. Achebe apparently wants to allow the reader to decide the matter for himself. Since the question has artistic as well as moral relevance, it may be well to investigate how Achebe manages to achieve this ambiguity.

In the first pages of the novel Achebe has Ezeulu ponder his role as a priest:

> Whenever Ezeulu considered the immensity of his power over the year and the crops and, therefore, over the people he wondered if it was real. It was true he named the day for the feast of the Pumpkin Leaves and for the New Yam feast;. but he did not choose the day...If he should refuse to name the day there would be no festival—no planting and no reaping. But could he refuse? No Chief Priest had ever refused. So it could not be done. He would not dare.
>
> Ezeulu was stung to anger by this as though his enemy had spoken it.
>
> "Take away that word *dare*," he replied to this enemy. "Yes I say take it away. No man in all Umuaro can stand up and say that I dare not. The woman who will bear the man who will say it has not yet been born."
>
> But this rebuke brought only momentary satisfaction. His mind still persisted in trying to look too closely at the nature of his power. What kind of power was it if everybody knew that it would never

> be used? Better to say that it was not there, that it was no more
> than the power in the anus of the proud dog who tried to put out a
> furnace with his puny fart. (3-4)

Ezeulu is thus introduced as a man tempted to test the limits of
his power. He wants to know if he has any real control over the
lives of his clansmen. His enemies, we soon learn, regard him as
an inordinately ambitious man. A rival priest asserts, "The man
who carries a deity is not a king. He is there to perform its ritual
and to carry sacrifice to it. But I have been watching this Ezeulu
for many years. He is a man of ambition; he wants to be king,
priest, diviner, all" (33). Even Ezeulu's oldest son Edogo suspects
that his father has already abused his priestly office by attempting
to influence Ulu's choice of his successor:

> Could it be that their father had deliberately sent Oduche to the
> religion of the white man so as to disqualify him for the priesthood
> of Ulu?...It was what anyone who knew Ezeulu would expect him
> to do. But was he not presuming too much? The choice of a priest
> lay with the deity. Was it likely that he would let the old priest
> force his hand? (113-14)

Moreover, at the end of the novel we learn that Ezeulu's people
interpret his fall as evidence that "Their god had taken sides
with them against his head-strong and ambitious priest and thus
upheld the wisdom of their ancestors—that no man however
great was greater than his people; that no man ever won
judgement against his clan" (287). Opinions like these lead us to
believe Ezeulu is guilty of *hubris* and responsible for his own
downfall.

But there is a countercurrent of opinion in the novel which
suggests that all of Ezeulu's actions are truly god-inspired. As
the priest of Ulu, he is thought to be "half-man half-spirit" (164,
166), someone incapable of taking any action offensive to his
god. Ezeulu's closest friend Akuebue does not doubt his absolute
religious integrity: "I know Ezeulu better than most people. He
is a proud man and the most stubborn person you know is only

his messenger; but he would not falsify the decision of Ulu. If he did it Ulu would not spare him to begin with" (266). When someone else remarks that a "priest like Ezeulu leads a god to ruin himself," Akuebue answers, "perhaps a god like Ulu leads a priest to ruin himself" (266). In support of Akuebue's belief that the old priest is not responsible for his actions, is the fact that Ezeulu feels betrayed by Ulu at the end, when his world collapses. Ezeulu apparently never once doubted that he was acting in his god's behalf.

But was Ezeulu sane? This question must be asked in the latter half of the novel when the priest visualizes himself as an "arrow in the bow of his god." Before his imprisonment he had acted responsibly in his religious office but afterward he was maniacally bent on punishing his people. Perhaps his imprisonment unhinged his mind. In prison he had had nightmares and had laid the plans for his "revenge" on his clan. He had told a kinsman, "I want to wrestle with my own people whose hand I know and who know my hand. I am going to challenge all those who have been poking their fingers into my face to come outside their gate and meet me in combat and whoever throws the other will strip him of his anklet" (221). This sounds like a personal vendetta and perhaps it was meant as one at first. But when Ezeulu gets home, he softens toward the neighbors and friends who welcome him back and begins to consider "the possibility of reconciliation or, if that was too much, of narrowing down the area of conflict." Suddenly he hears a voice:

> "Ta! Nwanu!" barked Ulu in his ear, as a spirit would in the ear of an impertinent human child. "Who told you that this was your own fight?"
>
> Ezeulu trembled and said nothing.
>
> "I say who told you that this was your own fight which you could arrange to suit you? You want to save your friends who brought you palm wine he-he-he-he-he!" laughed the deity the way spirits do—a dry, skeletal laugh. "Beware you do not come betwee

me and my victim or you may receive blows not meant for you!" (240-41)

After hearing this voice Ezeulu never again considers the possibility of a reconciliation with his people. He is obsessed with the idea of helping his god carry on the fight.

So the question remains: can Ezeulu be held responsible for his actions? Achebe, by presenting his priest-hero in an ambiguous light, avoids giving an answer. His intention is to explore "the relationship between a god and his priest...[and] this old question of who decides what shall be the wish of the gods" (Nkosi 21). He leaves the reader puzzling over these profound problems. As one critic, Clem Abiaziem Okafor, remarked in a perceptive essay on *Arrow of God*, Achebe raises very significant questions but he "is not a preacher and so he does not offer any cut and dried answer. He wants each individual to find his own way of coming to terms with the complexities of life" (214).

The religious drama in *Arrow of God* is played out against the backdrop of the colonial drama in Nigeria. Achebe is actually telling two stories at once, interweaving them with such skill that they cannot be separated. Ezeulu, a guardian of the old order, must fall before the new order can firmly establish itself. Missionaries and European administrative officials undermine the old priest's authority in the clan and thereby precipitate his fall. The forces of change, which Ezeulu had hoped to cope with via his mission-educated son, thus overwhelm him and transform his society. Europe's emissaries in Africa are shown to be culturally arrogant men with no real understanding of the people they have been sent to rule.

The stylistic difference between the language employed by British officials in Her Majesty's colonial service and that employed by Ibo villagers in *Arrow of God* serves to emphasize the vast cultural barriers that separate the colonizer from the colonized. In this way Achebe helps the reader to perceive how easily tragic misunderstanding and failures of communication could and did occur in colonial confrontations between Europe and Africa.

Achebe's major characters are complex living beings whose actions are also symbols in a schematic historical drama elucidating the human consequences of European colonialism in Africa. Achebe's fiction never fails to transcend the local and particular and enter realms of larger significance.

dventure and Self-Discovery in *Mission to Kala*

When young Jean-Marie Medza sets out on his mission to Kala, he whimsically imagines himself as a conquistador undertaking a "dangerous expedition into unknown and possibly hostile territory" (Beti 7) inhabited by "primitive, simple-minded tribes" (24). The image is ridiculous, for Medza is anything but heroic, Kala is only twenty-seven miles away, and the people he is going to visit are extremely friendly and related to him by blood. Yet it is true that he is entering a different world. Medza has spent most of his life closeted in cosmopolitan schools, where he has been force-fed the staples of Western education, but now he is about to venture into a remote hinterland, where book learning and urban colonial manners are virtually unknown. Naturally, he feels a bit nervous about living among his country cousins, for he imagines he will find it difficult to adjust to some of their outlandish customs. Like an arrogant visitor from a "higher" civilization—a conquistador, in fact—Medza tends to be incurably ethnocentric, viewing any deviation from his own cultural patterns as barbarous and uncouth.

Fortunately, Kala transforms him. His mission proves to be a profoundly enriching educational experience because it carries him inward as well as outward, taking him deep into hidden interior regions of his mind, which otherwise he would not have had the opportunity to explore. Medza's mission to Kala is an expedition into his own psyche, a voyage of self-discovery. After little more than a month there, he returns home a wiser, healthier man, having gained a better perspective on his own life by seeing how others live.

Of course, if the decision had been left to him, Medza probably would have never made the journey. Not being by nature an adventurer, and having failed the second part of his *baccalauréat* exams, he was in no mood to travel. He would have preferred to stay home and nurse his shattered schoolboy's ego by dutifully preparing for a second try at his exams. He has to be forced out of his shell by his cousin Niam and an old village patriarch, who insist that he go to Kala to retrieve Niam's runaway wife. Medza, never one to defy the authority of his elders, cannot refuse this assignment.

The nature of Medza's task is significant, for it introduces several important themes into the narrative. One of these is sexual freedom. Niam's wife is a libertine who has run off with many men in the past, but never before has she inconvenienced her husband by staying away such a long time. Although her previous affairs have given her a bad name in the neighborhood, Niam has always been willing to take her back to avoid the problem of searching for someone to replace her. But this time, after she has been gone for more than six months, Niam's domestic life is in disarray, so he feels compelled to begin negotiations with her father to seek her return. He claims to have the complete support of his village, explaining to Medza, "It isn't just my personal affair any longer. It's a tribal matter. My wife doesn't belong to me exclusively...she's tribal property" (19). In abandoning her husband, Niam's wife has challenged the notion that she is anyone's property and has questioned the right of her society to regulate her private life. She is a sexual rebel, a free and independent spirit unfettered by conventional moral codes.

She is also a young person resisting domination and exploitation by an older generation. Niam has treated her abominably, not only working her "worse than a dog" (14) but constantly insulting her as well. She has been a disappointment to him as a wife because by failing to produce children, she has not lived up to her side of the marriage contract. This wins her the contempt of the entire adult community. It is not surprising that a young woman in such unhappy circumstances should seek release from the miseries of her home life by becoming involved in romantic affairs with strangers. Nor is it surprising that she should run away. After all, she knows what the consequences of her flight will be. Her lazy husband eventually will realize that he cannot get along without someone to take care of his house and farm; he will therefore pursue her by sending an emissary to confront her father; then she will have the option of either agreeing to a divorce or resuming her household duties. She has no intention of breaking off from Niam completely, but she wants to be able to return on her own terms, despite having defied his authority and scandalized the village. Her behavior reflects her determination to assert her individuality by exercising some control over her own destiny and by defining her own life-style.

Medza's role in this marital squabble is that of a conscripted advocate for the *status quo ante*. His job is to present Niam's case to the errant girl's father and demand her return. In other words, he functions as an enforcer of traditional moral codes, an agent of social conformity. This turns out to be an ironic role for Medza to play because he himself gradually changes into a rebellious nonconformist. Indeed, his struggle for self-liberation roughly parallels that of Niam's wife.

At the outset Medza is very much in need of emancipation. He has grown up under the heavy thumb of his father, a stern, unloving old man who sends him away to boarding schools at a tender age to keep him out of trouble. Although Medza works very hard at his studies and carries home many certificates and diplomas, he is never permitted to feel that he is anything other than a colossal disappointment as a son. Having failed his *baccalauréat* exams, he knows his father will be furious and dreads facing him. Going off to Kala will at least postpone the stormy confrontation for a few days. Thus, though he gives the appearance of reluctantly agreeing to represent his community's interests, Medza obviously has an ulterior motive for undertaking his mission. He is subconsciously seeking a release from his repressive home environment and a temporary escape from his father's wrath.

Medza's complete psychological liberation is eventually achieved through sexual initiation. When he arrives in Kala, he quickly learns that this is a community where it is not at all unusual for young, unmarried men and women to sleep together. Though he is desperately eager to take advantage of this unfamiliar situation, he fears the humiliation of being exposed as a virgin, especially since his new village friends seem to assume that any normal city boy must be a veteran lecher. His cousin Zambo, anxious to make him feel at home, pushes the most desirable girl in all of Kala into his bedroom, but nothing comes of it because Medza is so afraid of disappointing her that he cannot work up the courage even to hold her hand. To save face and avoid further embarrassment, he pretends he is tired of experienced women and now wants someone young and pure. Zambo obliges by producing Edima. It is Edima who finally leads Medza out of his state of innocence. After his sexual initiation Medza begins to behave like a man.

The first sign of his newfound maturity is his willingness to stand up to his father. Before going to Kala, Medza had been entirely dominated by this "private dictator" and "domestic tyrant" (187). He had obediently gone to school, obediently learned his lessons, obediently refrained from any behavior his father might have considered unrespectable. As a consequence, he had never grown up and asserted himself as an individual. It is only after he has entered a totally different environment that Medza begins to see his life in a new light and to question the alien system of values by which he has been forced to live. He realizes that all his natural impulses have been thwarted or suppressed during his school years, that he has been confined in a mental straitjacket and made a prisoner of Western education. He soon comes to envy the less cerebral life of his village companions.

> I'd have given all the diplomas in the world to swim like Duckfoot Johnny, or dance like the Boneless Wonder, or have the sexual experience of Petrus Son-of-God, or throw an assegai like Zambo...I

saw this freedom as the most precious possession I could acquire, and realised at the same time that in all likelihood I should never have it. Without being aware of it, I was no more than a sacrifice on the altar of Progress and Civilisation. My youth was slipping away, and I was paying a terrible price for—well, for *what*? Having gone to school, at the decree of my all-powerful father? Having been chained to my books when most children of my age were out playing games? (71, 76).

It is Medza's recognition of the terrible price he has had to pay for Westernization that leads him to revolt against his father, but he does not have the strength of character to carry out his revolt until he has overcome his fear of women. He must prove himself a man in bed before he can defy parental authority. Fornication sets him free.

Edima, the girl who helps to liberate him, is a true child of nature. Innocent, uncomplicated, "sharp and fresh as a ripening orange" (163), she has a wholesome yet earthy kind of beauty, which Medza finds extraordinarily appealing. At first he is so eager for erotic adventure that he can view her only as an opportunity for sexual exploitation, but as he comes to know her better, he begins to develop an appreciation for her rustic simplicity and to respect her as an individual. His lust then subsides, to be replaced by feelings of brotherly tenderness, and eventually he realizes that he loves her. They are united, first surreptitiously with the help of Zambo, and then formally by means of a surprise marriage ceremony arranged by her father. Since Edima represents all that is good in traditional village life, Medza's acceptance of her as his wife is symbolic of his reorientation of values. He leaves Kala a profoundly changed man, having learned to accept his African heritage.

Before going to Kala, Medza had been almost completely deracinated by his education; he thought and acted like a Frenchman who accidentally had been born black. Much of the humor in his narrative derives from the fact that he is a detribalized African reentering a traditional tribal milieu and responding to it in a typical European fashion. He regards the inhabitants of Kala as "up-country bushmen" (23) who delight in childish sports, picturesque ceremonies, and foolish customs. He believes that such primitive, simple-minded savages cannot be expected to have high principles or enlightened views, for they are uncivilized creatures totally devoid of culture and intellectual refinement. Medza does not manage to rid himself of all these prejudices during his stay in Kala, but his experiences constantly force him to reexamine his assumptions about traditional African society. In doing so, he also has to reevaluate his own upbringing.

Ironically, Medza is lionized in Kala because of his education. The villagers never tire of asking him questions about what he has learned at school, although at first he is a bit annoyed about being put through the ordeal of another oral examination. When he snaps at one particularly insistent interviewer, an old man intercedes and tries to soothe him by pointing out, "For us *you* are the white man—you are the only person who can explain these mysteries to us...If you refuse, we've probably lost our only chance of ever being able to learn the white man's wisdom" (77-78). Medza gives in and soon finds himself the star attraction in a traveling educational road show that makes the rounds of virtually every household in Kala. It is during these nightly interrogations that he discovers how little he actually knows about some of the subjects he has studied so assiduously at school. The superficiality of his education depresses him, especially when he considers what he has had to forfeit for it.

> My resentment against schools and educational systems mounted steadily as the days passed by. I saw a school as a kind of giant ogre, swallowing young boys, digesting them slowly, vomiting them up again sucked dry of all their youthful essence, mere skeletons. (81)

Such insights put Medza in the mood to rebel. Through his efforts to teach others "the white man's wisdom" (78), he learns so much about himself that he wants to alter his life-style drastically—to seek out those physical experiences he has missed and purge himself of the mental blocks and neuroses that have always crippled him psychologically. For him, Kala has been an awakening, a real education.

He cannot, of course, turn the clock back completely and erase all his earlier life experiences. The past still has a firm grip on him, and as he returns home, he begins to fear how his father will react to the news that he is now married to an uneducated country girl. Though he fortifies himself with palm-wine to achieve an artificial bravado, he never manages to summon sufficient courage to reveal what happened to him in Kala. So the evening before Edima and her wedding party are to arrive in town, Medza decides that he has no alternative other than to run away. He knows that it would be absolutely impossible for him to lead a normal married life in his father's household with a girl like Edima. Indeed, his father has given him such terrible complexes about sex that, as Medza puts it, "the mere notion of making love to Edima in the same house where he was sleeping was enough to turn me completely impotent" (197-98). To escape the emasculating influence of his father, Medza must sever all ties with his past.

What is much more difficult for him is to sever his new ties with Edima. He views her as the essence of purity and innocence, the embodiment of all his ideals; yet he recognizes that his education has made the two of them incompatible as husband and wife. They are too far apart intellectually to be happy if bound together in any kind of permanent union. He must desert her in order to achieve his true independence.

This desertion represents a rejection of traditional African society. Although Medza no longer looks down upon illiterate villagers as primitive savages, he is not blind to some of their human imperfections. He is aware that both his uncle and Edima's father exploited him while he was in Kala, and also that Edima herself may have been involved in the conspiracy to trap him into a surprise marriage. In other words, Medza recognizes that he had as little control over his affairs in Kala as he now has at home. Old men are still trying to take advantage of him and to dominate even the most private regions of his personal life. It is only fitting that in his rebellion against social tyranny Medza should reject traditional as well as modern forms of oppression.

The price of Medza's freedom is his total alienation. He realizes he can reside neither in his father's world nor in Edima's, so he spends the rest of his life wandering from place to place in search of a "true purity" which he thinks he is "probably too old ever to find" (205). Looking back, he remembers his mission to Kala as the turning point in his life, for it helped him to discover many truths, not the least of which was

> the discovery—made by contact with the country folk of Kala, those quintessential caricatures of the "colonised" African—that the tragedy which our nation is suffering today is that of a man left to his own devices in a world which does not belong to him, which he has not made and does not understand. It is the tragedy of a man bereft of any intellectual compass. (205-06)

This insight into modern African life reveals that Medza, though still searching for an elusive goal, has found his true bearings in a world in which everyone else is irretrievably lost. Like a conquistador, he has returned from a great adventure with the richest of treasures: a better understanding of himself and of his place in an absurd universe.

South Africa's First Indian Novel

Behold the Earth Mourns by Ansuyah R. Singh is a forgotten piece of South African fiction. Unlisted in bibliographies of South African literature, unavailable in even the best-stocked libraries and bookshops, unnoticed by literary commentators for more than thirty years, it is now virtually an erased text, one that has all but disappeared from sight. Yet its dust jacket states that "this is the first novel by a South African Indian." Perhaps it is time to restore some visibility to this vanished pioneer.

The back flap of the book tells us that

> Ansuyah R. Singh, born in Durban, is a graduate in Medicine of the University of Edinburgh. She has travelled extensively in Europe and India and has worked in many hospitals, and for a while was in private practice.
>
> In 1954 she obtained a Council for Scientific & Industrial Research Bursary and subsequently in 1956 joined the Department of Social, Preventive and Family Medicine, Faculty of Medicine, University of Natal and Institute of Family and Community Health where she now holds the post of Senior Lecturer and Family Physician.
>
> Besides Medicine, her interests lie in Social Service, Music and Amateur Theatre. She has portrayed the leading roles of Shrimati in Rabindranath Tagore's *Natir Puja*, as Sakuntala in Kalidas' play and several others.
>
> She writes in *Jyothi*, the quarterly journal of the Rama-Krishna Centre of South Africa and has to her credit Medical Research articles.
>
> This is her first effort in fiction.

A photo above this biographical blurb shows an attractive young woman in modest but elegant attire, looking to her right.

The book appears to have been privately published. The last page carries the notice that it was "printed in the Union of South Africa by Cape Times Limited, Cape Town," but no publisher's name is given, and no date of publication is recorded. However, a dedication "to South Africa on the centenary of the arrival of the Indians in the country" would place its appearance around 1960. The front flyleaf offers a brief summary of some of the novel's unique characteristics:

> Set partly in South Africa and in India, this is a novel of a well-to-do Indian family, who participate in passive resistance and whose domestic affairs reveal the stresses and strains in character with Indian family life. It carries an authentic and rare stamp of a quasi-mystical and quasi-poetic imagination. The South African Indians are among the most colourful strands in our multi-coloured society with a philosophy of life which has enabled them to endure many buffets and restraints. What that philosophy is and how near it lies to Christianity in its occasional use of Satyagraha shines through the gentle pages of the story.
>
> From the ancient Vedantic teachings Mahatma Gandhi translated this philosophy into a living force giving it reality and purpose in modern times.
>
> The reader may find the names strange at first, but the Nirvani family, including Srenika, the man who goes to prison for his beliefs, holds interest. The story is pensive, yet somehow in tune with the floweriness of Indian thought, its obscurities and its reluctance to take action.
>
> It is the expression of the feelings among a highly civilised minority which has rarely been portrayed.

The story is certainly an interesting amalgam, being both characteristically South African in its political concerns and characteristically Indian in its philosophical outlook. At one level it is a tale of material dispossession, racial discrimination and bureaucratic cruelty—classic anti-apartheid themes worked out within the context of Indian life in Durban. At another level it is a simple love story set in two dissimilar worlds—South Africa and India—where distance complicates courtship and marriage, leading to unhappiness, separation and domestic distress. The private drama is played out against the backdrop of public events in South Africa in the 1940s and 1950s.

The novel opens with the prosperous Nirvani family being forced to leave their comfortable seven-acre homestead on the outskirts of Durban and move into a much smaller house in a less desirable location. They and others like them are victims of newly enacted laws aimed at residential racial segregation. According to Julie Frederikse,

> The Asiatic Land Tenure and Indian Representation Act of 1946—known as the Ghetto Act—prohibited Indians from buying land and occupying property except in certain 'exempted areas'. It was this legislation that gave rise to the passive resistance campaign. The Group Areas Act of 1950 designated separate urban residential areas for each race group, and also gave rise to great resistance. (36)

Krishandutt, the older Nirvani brother who runs the family's business enterprises, accepts the injustice of forced removal fatalistically, feeling helpless to overturn oppressive laws, but his younger brother Srenika is bent on expressing his opposition to the new system through passive resistance. He wants to follow Gandhi's example by pursuing Satyagraha (defined in the novel's three-page glossary of Indian terms as "the path of truth and non-violence"), thereby sacrificing himself as a martyr to a worthwhile cause. The brothers argue out their differences, articulating positions that must have been typical of the divided Indian community in South Africa at the time:

> "Srenika—I cannot understand you. Life's pattern evolves slowly. No one can change these things that make us suffer, rapidly—overnight."

> "That is so, Krishandutt. It is not just going into prison. It is not becoming a martyr, or a hero whichever way you would like to put it. Its..."
>
> "Srenika, you forget that we are only part of a vast plan—the design of God. We are but one small unit in the unappreciable universality of man, and this too is based on laws, the laws of creation and destruction, the pattern of action and reaction."
>
> "I am interested at this moment in my action, and my choice. I am real. I accept and am part of that great universe you describe to me. I want to do—and to do that which my conscience feels is right. I want to destroy that which is wrong, not by another action of wrongness, but by my own sacrifice and practice of truth." (8)

The consequence of Srenika's highmindedness is predictable: he is arrested, imprisoned, punished with hard labor and inadequate food, and thrown into solitary confinement. Yet when someone outside offers to pay his fine in order to get him released, Srenika refuses to come out, preferring to suffer further indignities and pains. He will not compromise his conscience or display moral cowardice.

The second part of the novel concerns the major event in Srenika's life after prison: his marriage to Yagesvari Jivan-Sinha, a beautiful young woman from a well-to-do family in Bombay. His brother and sister-in-law had wanted him to marry the daughter of a family friend, arguing that "the association goes back to the home of our family in North India. They are the same caste, Kshatriya." But Srenika abruptly dismisses this suggestion:

> "Do you still want to consider caste? Do you still believe in its abominable atrocity? I cannot. I have renounced that background almost from my cradle."
>
> "Oh yes, but when it comes to marriage, and the making of a new family, the right two people have to come together. This is our tradition, our culture. We cannot rebuke it."
>
> "I do not want to rebuke it. I want to forsake it. I believe in individual merit—the inherent worth of a man." (34)

Besides, Srenika has his heart set on Yagesvari whom he had met and fallen in love with on a visit to India the year before. She is considered by his family to be an acceptable match, so negotiations for her hand are initiated discreetly by relatives. Yagesvari's father has some reservations about the prospect of her living in South Africa, saying, "I would find it most painful to send her to any place where her dignity as a human being, where her nobility as a person would be ignored or wounded" (53), but eventually he is won over. Yagesvari herself is very receptive to the proposal, imagining "the excitement of being in a new country and the adventure of starting life with someone she had not known intimately" (55). So wedding plans are made, and Srenika, with the help of a lawyer friend, obtains papers enabling him to leave for India.

Wedding arrangements proceed smoothly until apartheid raises its ugly head once again. The South African regime passes a new regulation prohibiting Indian wives from entry into South Africa.[1] This news throws Srenika's family into turmoil. His brother Krishandutt is shocked:

> "By the Great God Brahma, this cannot be. This will dishonour us in the eyes of God, and our people if anything happens to interfere with Srenika's marriage to Yagesvari. Is it not natural that a man, when he marries, can live with his wife in his country? Is it not right to marry from choice? This to me is the most important protection—this freedom to choose a wife and live in one's own country." (87)

When the news gets to India, Yagesvari's father is alarmed enough to consider calling off the wedding, but his wife insists that they honor their original agreement, even if it means that Yagesvari will be without citizenship in South Africa:

> "There is a greater citizenship than the one that man creates. It is a deep communication of the self in God. If we understand this then our relationship to one another, to the sentiments of country, to

people is without any barrier. It does not matter whether one has citizenship but it does matter if one is incarnated in the human form and relates with himself and his fellow beings with harmony and Godliness. I cannot oppose this marriage. It has been our desire and it came through the love of our two children. I beg you to allow it to be consecrated with a spirit of goodwill and blessing." (90)

Yasgesvari's father again relents, guided by his wife's good faith and judgment. In due course the marriage is solemnized.

The real problems begin when the newlyweds fly into Johannesburg and are told by an immigration officer that Yagesvari will not be permitted to disembark in the country. They appeal the decision, and she is granted a temporary permit enabling her to remain in Durban until her case can be reviewed by immigration authorities.

After this rather rocky start, Yagesvari tries to settle down to life with her in-laws. They accept her warmly, but some of her ways are strange to them, and some of theirs are equally foreign to her. Indian women in South Africa do not have the same liberties in dress or manner as women in India do. Also, Yagesvari is not accustomed to being barred from public places because she is not white. Small tensions arise, putting further strain on the marriage. Yagesvari wants them to have a home of their own instead of living in Krishandutt's house. She becomes homesick, moody, and unhappy. Her attitude improves only after she learns that she is pregnant.

However, the South African Government's enactment of apartheid legislation continues its relentless course. A radio broadcast informs them that "No wife of a marriage contracted by Indians outside South Africa will be allowed to remain or enter the country" (147), and soon they receive an official letter to this effect. Srenika is hurt and confused:

"I can't understand this. I am part of this country. I have caused her no harm, no suffering. I have been and am constructive. By my very nature I have contributed to her all that has been good in me. My loyalty has been unquestionable. By depriving me of my wife I am being rejected, blamed, accused, maligned. The most important thing in my life is threatened." (150)

They consider challenging the decree in the courts, but Yagesvari, feeling she cannot bear any further torment, decides it would be better for her to return to India.

There, while husband and wife are separated, their daughter is born. Yagesvari yearns for Srenika, and he pines for her. Her father suggests that Srenika repatriate to India and take over his business, but Yagesvari tells him that this is impossible:

"Srenika will never accept the fruit of your harvest. He and many like him have started something in a small river that must flood in the heavy rains, and when it becomes a tempestuous torrent, it will grow rapidly in a swift current seawards. Because it is like this my place is with Srenika." (175)

She books a passage to Trieste on a ship that will dock in Durban, intending to rejoin her husband by illegally entering South Africa.

The plan works but only for a day. She and her child are tracked down, arrested and taken to jail. Srenika is allowed to post bail for the child, but Yagesvari is put into a cell with common criminals. Distraught, she attempts suicide. Her cellmates rescue her, but she is no longer her normal self. Srenika is permitted by prison officials to take her home, where she begins to recover and then relapses with a devouring fever. Srenika feels great remorse:

"Oh Yagesvari, what have I done to you? You have suffered so much for me. You have been thrown against the swift current of emotions, of people, of life. Instead you should have had peace where your beauty would have blossomed with utter radiance. But my little wife I love you and wanted you more than life itself."

"Yes Srenika. You once told me that it is hard to understand. Now I do. Life in its brief space of time unfolds many fashions of existence. All our trials experiences, and people are puppets in a dream. The Unknown Hand pulls the strings in the drama—the illusion to which our mind and our emotions play. In all this my love alone remains to banish from my wearied heart cruel pain, and my soul is not seared." (200)

At this point the story ends. The final lines of the novel, a poetic quatrain, suggest that Yagesvari suddenly dies.

Despite this rather melodramatic conclusion, *Behold the Earth Mourns* can be recommended as a book that depicts with sensitivity and compassion the tenor of Indian life in South Africa under apartheid. The fortitude, stoicism and equanimity with which the Nirvani family copes with the hardships of living in an unjust society bespeak an abiding faith in a divine plan for human existence. Adversity is something to be endured, accepted, absorbed. Those who suffer may rebel, as Srenika does, but they must do so in a controlled, principled, nonviolent fashion, obedient to the dictates of a higher truth. Satyagraha is the only spiritually pure form of resistance to social evils.

This is not to say that other alternatives to ending oppression in South Africa are not discussed in the novel. Srenika has an African friend, Serete, who joins the passive resistance campaign and also goes to prison but who angrily rejects Srenika's philosophizing as "babble...high level cheap bla."

"Do you think you can turn the fear that hurts within me into a quiet suffering and expect repentance from whoever causes it? Do you think you can retard and push back my personality, my rights as a human being and expect me not to suffer? Do you think our suffering is going to cure other people's evil?...People like you Srenika spoil things for us and there is no strength in this type of talk." (18)

Serete favors a more active form of resistance.

Most of the whites Srenika encounters are part of the government machinery of oppression—police officers, immigration officials, prison superintendents, and the like—but he also has a few white friends who are genuinely concerned about his welfare. There are several Coloured characters in the book too, neighbors whose presence suggests that the Indian community is not completely isolated from other ethnic groups. Indeed, there is a rather free mixing of races in Durban, a natural pluralism that conveys the impression that forced segregation simply does not make sense. Apartheid is an aberration that disrupts people's lives, destroying all potential for collective social harmony.

But these overtly political threads in the story are subordinated to the larger theme of transcendent love. Srenika and Yagesvari are not radicalized or embittered by their experiences; they rail against the man-made cruelties they are compelled to suffer, but in the end they accept their fate, secure in the knowledge that their steadfast love has enabled them to overcome petty worldly cares. Even in the most thwarting external circumstances, they have managed to achieve an inner peace.

Behold the Earth Mourns has some shortcomings as a novel, but because it succeeds in conveying a notion of Indian life in South Africa during the era of apartheid, it serves as a valuable record of how members of a distinctive minority group viewed their disadvantages and responsibilities in a racist society. Further, it affords insight into some of the principles that have guided Indian responses to blatant oppression, injustice and violence. But perhaps more than anything else, it reveals the deep spirituality with which Indians, whether in India or South Africa, approach matters of the heart. This tender love story set in a hateful environment is therefore a worthy precursor of the Indian writing that gradually emerged in South Africa in the 1970s and 1980s, a literature that continued to be dominated by ideas that were simultaneously political and personal.[2]

[1] This incident was based on a real event. According to Mabel Palmer, in the mid-1950s the South African Government abrogated one of the provisions of the Smuts-Gandhi Agreement of 1914 that allowed Indians domiciled in South Africa to bring their wives and children from India: "Obstacles have been placed in the way of a number of Indian women coming to Durban from India to join their husbands. The legality of this prohibition is open to grave doubt." (73)

[2] For a brief survey of this literature, see Alvarez-Péreyre.

John Bruin: South African Enigma in Texas

After delivering a lecture on "The South African Poet and His Landscape" one sun-washed Texas morning, I was approached by a buxom coed who asked if I knew the poetry of John Bruin. "No, can't say I do," I confessed. "John Bruin. Is he American, English, Russian? His name sounds somewhat grizzly."

"No, sir," she groaned, wincing at the pun. "He's South African and he published his first book of poems here in Texas."

"Really? How bizarre! And how many centuries ago did he do this?" I was still trying to conceal the enormity of my ignorance behind transparent jokes.

"Just a few months ago. Troubadour Press in Del Valle brought it out."

There was a faint tinkle in my mind. Several weeks before, at a faculty cocktail party held on a brick patio surrounding a mammoth barbecue pit, someone had been regaling a covey of bra-less miniskirted teaching assistants with tales about Troubadour Press and its eccentric octogenarian founder, S.K. Skoonman. I remember them all wobbling with guffaws and titters upon hearing the titles published by this myopically regional press. "But I thought Troubadour Press only published books about barbecue sauce and things like that," I said.

"So did I," she replied without so much as a quiver, "but I found *this* over at the Grackle." She held up a copy of *Thoughts Abroad* by John Bruin, a 28-page pamphlet of poems with a striking line drawing of a pensive, agonized head on the cover. The back cover gave some information on the author:

John Bruin is a South African currently teaching and writing outside his country. He is, as his work shows, both widely travelled and homesick. He has already been published in many magazines, in various countries and languages, and has a steadily growing reputation as perhaps one of the first South African poets to achieve international recognition. Two books of his poetry are due to appear shortly; for fuller information write to Troubadour Press.

"Why have I never heard of this poet?" I mumbled into my beard, letting my own thoughts rove abroad. The coed brought me to my senses by snatching back her book and bobbing off to her next class. I immediately went over to the Grackle and bought my own copy for dollar.

Walking slowly, I was able to read most of the poems on the way back to my office. Then I spent the rest of the morning rereading them in silent amazement and wondering about the identity of the poet. These were some of the finest South African poems I had seen, but this was the first time I had come across the name John Bruin. If he was so widely published and well-known, why hadn't I encountered his work elsewhere? I leafed through several South African anthologies in my office just to see if I might have missed him on earlier readings, but his name couldn't be found in any of them. Could John Bruin be the pseudonym of another poet, one who perhaps was not even South African? It might just be S.K. Skoonman himself, I thought, for the old man had achieved a measure of local notoriety as a verse-maker and was known to have published much of his own work under fictitious names. He had already brought out two small volumes of his own poetry via Troubadour Press and maybe this was a method of disguising a third. But why should a flag-waving Texas aboriginal (his first book of poems was called *Remember the Alamo!*) pretend to be a nostalgic South African? On the other hand, if John Bruin were real, why should "one of the first South African poets to achieve international recognition" choose the imprint of an obscure publishing house in Del Valle, Texas? Intrigued by these questions, I placed a long distance call to Troubadour Press and arranged to interview Skoonman the following weekend.

Then I went back to reading the poems. There were twenty-six of them, all quite short. Each was set on its own page and followed by a different place name. The names themselves were fascinating for they came from all over the world—Johannesburg, Stockholm, Rome, New Delhi, Sydney, London, Belfast, Fiji, Grenoble, Tehran, Dubrovnik—and the poems gave evidence of having been either written or inspired in these widely scattered places. John Bruin obviously was a member of the international jet-set.

Most of these globe-girdling poems, however, took the shape of memories or reflections on South Africa. These were truly the "thoughts abroad" of an itinerant poet heartsick for his homeland. In several poems Bruin personifies his land as a lover from whom he has been parted—first physically, then spiritually. The opening poem announces this theme of separation by recollecting the poet's last intimate contact with his loved one:

When last I ranged and revelled all your length
I vowed to savour your most beauteous curves
with such devout and lingering delight
that they would etch themselves into my brain
to comfort me throughout the prisoned night.

But waking early in the frowsty dawn
and finding you dishevelled and unkempt
my heart arose as though you showed your best
—and then I wryly knew myself to be
the slave of an habituated love.

The poem is signed "Jbg/Mbabane," as if to suggest the poet was already in the process of leaving his country at the time of writing.

Many of the later poems describe the poet's reactions in adjusting to new places, new climates, new peoples, new responsibilities, new moods. But usually there is an undercurrent of retrospection, of looking back toward the world he has left. In a London suburb he writes:

> November sunlight silvers my grimy panes,
> suffuses the gruel-grey sky
> and gleams on the cold woodwork;
>
> such wan luminescence
> might as well not be,
> lacks all virtue, is devoid of warmth
>
> while Southwards in a steady blaze
> like a sheet of molten lead heat pours down
> and the world glows, while here I pine.

The poet does not always picture his homeland as a realm of glorious sunshine and warmth, however. More frequently he sees it as a cold, hard, dark island, a place of confinement and death where men rot in their insularity. This harsh image reinforces the poet's determination to remain in voluntary exile and to continually strive for the liberation of the human spirit. Circling the earth, he ardently seeks fresh challenges and personal commitments, new modes of effective communication with his fellow man. And the strain of this quest eventually cools his youthful passions, alienating him from his former mistress.

> I am out of love with you for now;
> cold-sodden in my misery
> your contours and allurements
> cannot move me:
>
> I murmur old endearments to revive
> our old familiar glow again
> —like sapless autumn leaves
> they rasp in vain.

You have asked too much of me:
fond-fool, bereft I cling
unloving, to remembered love
and the spring.

In turning away from the "contours and allurements" that once moved him, the poet symbolically progresses from narrow, parochial concerns to a more universal outlook. His unrewarding early love for his land is transmuted in the course of time and world experience to a profound sympathy and affection for all people everywhere. The last poem in the booklet ends with the lines:

all the world is mine and to love
and all of its humankind.

The homesick poet has finally found a new and larger home.

The poetry was undeniably South African yet unique in its subtle renderings of certain characteristic moods and themes. The image of the poet as a tormented paramour in spiritual exile, the portrayal of the object of affection as seductively beautiful but cold, cruel and unreasonably demanding, the schizoid ambivalence between love and hate, the enlightenment gained by contact with the outside world—these commonplaces in South African poetry were handled with unusual sensitivity by John Bruin. Here was a poet who stood squarely in the mainstream of his nation's poetic tradition and still had something new to contribute. Here was an original voice singing a medley of old songs but articulating them with more feeling than anyone had ever done before. To whom did this impressive voice belong? That was the question I wanted to put to S.K. Skoonman.

I had been warned that the old man was a character straight out of the Old West so I half expected to find him in chaps and spurs, oiling a six-shooter or shoeing a mustang while somewhere in the background contented ranch-hands crooned cowboy songs around an open campfire. That stock Hollywood scenario quickly vanished only to be replaced by another when I pulled up in front of the Troubadour Press office, a neat two-storey stone rectangle with saloon-style swinging doors. "Used to be a prison," shouted a bewhiskered replica of Walt Whitman on the front porch, pointing at the barred windows on the upper floor. He was dressed in soiled blue denim coveralls, a threadbare T-shirt, and ink-spangled red boots. "We keep all our printing equipment up there now. Keeps it out of the hands of left-wing vigilantes. They were hopping mad when I published that book on Texas patriotism. Threatened to napalm my shop." His whiskers rearranged themselves into a smile.

"Mr. Skoonman, I presume," I said somewhat lamely as I contorted my way out of my Porsche.

"None other," he replied, shaking my hand with unoctogenarian vigor. His wrinkled eyes gleamed. "You must be the professor who teaches African literature up there at the University. I thought I might be seeing you if *Thoughts Abroad* ever fell into your hands. What do you think of John Bruin?"

"I think he's the greatest South African poet I've ever read. Who in the world is he?"

"Hard to tell for sure," he replied, scratching his head with a grimy knuckle. "Said John Bruin wasn't his real name but wouldn't admit who he was. He came through here, banjo on his back, about six months ago and claimed he was doing a walking tour of the U.S. Said he had danced and sung his way through most of the world since leaving South Africa. He had even published a couple other books of poems on his travels, but I gathered these were done on small presses like my own for he seemed proud of the fact that they hadn't received much distribution.

"Why should he be proud of that? I got the impression from the blurb on *Thoughts Abroad* that we was pretty well known."

"Yes, I believe he really is, but perhaps not so much for his poetry. I think he must have had a good reason for travelling and writing incognito. He said he did not want to offend certain people in South Africa by publishing anything under his real name."

"Was he black, by any chance?" I thought perhaps I had gained a clue to his identity.

Skoonman laughed abruptly. "Oh, no, not at all. He was a bit tanned from his travels, but he was a lot whiter than I am," he grinned, showing me his ink-stained palms. "No, he's not a revolutionary nut, if that's what you mean. I wouldn't have published him if he were, even though his poetry is truly first-rate. No, I think he's a blue blood from one of the well-known families in South Africa. He may have relatives in the Government or in the gold or diamond business down there. I don't suppose such a young man could have made his way around the world unless he were independently wealthy. He said he works as a teacher every now and then, but he sure couldn't afford all that jet travel on a teacher's salary. He must have a pot of money stashed away somewhere. I have a pet theory that he was a successful young business executive of some sort but then decided to chuck it all and bum around the world 'doing his thing,' which happens to be writing poetry. I like men like that because I did the same thing myself when I was young."

"Did you ever get to South Africa on your travels?" I asked, curious to find out if he had any acquaintance with Bruin's native landscape.

"Never. Furthest south I got in Africa was Lambaréné, where I visited Schweitzer. I wanted to get to Cape Town because, believe it or not, my great-grandfather had come from there, but *my* pot of money had run dry by the time I reached Gabon. Then the first World War broke out and changed everything, so I ended up fighting the Germans in Togo."

We talked about his travels and war experiences for a while before returning to Bruin's poetry. "Why do you suppose Bruin agreed to let you publish his poetry?" I wanted to know.

"*Agreed* to *let* me? Why, he suggested it himself! I think he rather liked the name of my press because he fancied himself as something of a modern-day troubadour, which he sure enough is. In fact, he may have deliberately sought me out because he wanted his book of poems to carry the name Troubadour Press. When he heard that I had South African ancestors, he grew almost ecstatic, and we talked long into the night about where they had come from and what they had done there. He took a great interest in my genealogy, and this led me to suspect he was from a fairly aristocratic family. He said he knew quite a few South Africans in Cape Town and Johannesburg with names like Skoonman. It was four o'clock in the morning before he left, and he returned the next day to settle all the business details related to his book. I haven't seen him since. He said he was going west and would write me when he had a permanent address, but I haven't heard from him yet. I don't even know if he has seen a copy of *Thoughts Abroad*. He seemed content to leave everything in my hands because he regarded me as a 'countryman' of his. A real gentleman, he was, and far and away the best poet I have ever published."

"Who else have you published?"

"Mostly Texas poets—Hyman Doubleday, Steve Russell, Sam Gees, Chuck L. Ralson, myself. That's about all so far. A few others will come out later this year. I also publish cookbooks featuring local dishes and books about Texas and the Southwest. C'mon up and I'll show you the warehouse."

Upstairs there were shelves filled with books about Texas armadillos, Texas dungbeetles, Texas desert flowers, prize-winning Texas recipes, Indian pottery, and organic fertilizers. Some were handsomely bound and lavishly illustrated, but most of those concerned with poetry were slim pamphlets of no more than 48 pages. Skoonman obviously earned his bread and butter on the expensive books and published poetry just for the fun (or love) of it. He was a character all right, but he also *had* character and I admired him for that.

As we came down the stairs I asked if he was planning to publish the two forthcoming volumes of Bruin's poetry mentioned on the back cover of *Thoughts Abroad*.

"No, Bruin told me he had already made arrangements with big publishers in New York and London for those books. Said they'd be coming out in the next couple of years and would probably have his real name on them. He believed he would be able to drop his anonymity then for there wouldn't be anyone left to offend in South Africa. He wouldn't explain what he meant by that. I figure maybe he's got a rich uncle or father who's on his deathbed down there and he doesn't want to upset the old guy with a family scandal. There are people like that, you know. People who think it's scandalous for a man to waste time writing poetry. My parents were that way too, and I didn't write under the name Skoonman until they were dead and gone. Maybe I'm just projecting my life experiences onto John Bruin, but I can't help it. I felt a real kinship for that young man."

"Think you'll hear from him again?"

"Yes, I'm sure I will someday, for he said he'd write as soon as he got settled. He struck me as an honest fellow, a man of his word, and I believe everything he told me was the gospel truth."

"Even the stuff about his name?"

"Especially that. Why should a man lie about a pseudonym? You don't think his name actually *is* John Bruin, do you? Have you got any idea what his real name might be?"

I shook my head and smiled. "Until this afternoon I thought there was an outside chance it might be S.K. Skoonman."

The whiskers were split by a sharp cackle. "I'd be flattered," the old man laughed, "if I thought you had read any of my verse before making that statement. I'm just a Texas poet who writes for his friends. John Bruin is a South African who writes for the whole world."[1]

---

[1] For those who haven't been able to read between the lines of this fable, it can now be revealed that John Bruin was a pseudonym for Dennis Brutus, who subsequently reprinted the poems in *Thoughts Abroad* as part of his collected verse in *A Simple Lust* (1973). S.K. Skoonman never existed, but Troubadour Press did, having been established as a vehicle to circumvent the Pretoria regime's efforts to prohibit publication and dissemination of Brutus's writings in South Africa. For further details on this ruse, see Lindfors, "Dennis Brutus, Texas Poet."

THOUGHTS ABROAD

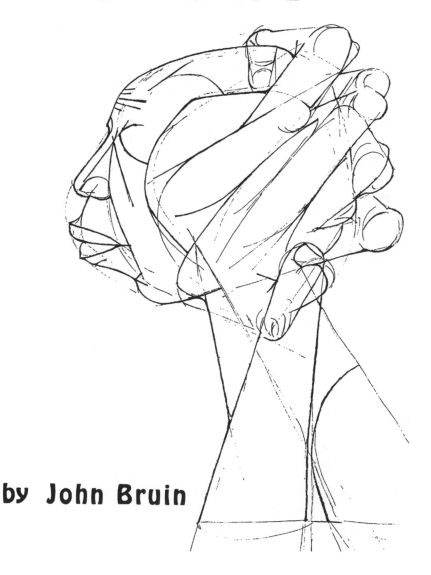

by John Bruin

Pre-Texts

Armah's Groton Essays

After Ayi Kwei Armah finished his secondary education at Achimota School in Accra, he spent an extra year at Groton School in Groton, Massachusetts before entering Harvard University in the fall of 1960. He was the first African student to attend Groton, an elite, boys' boarding school that had admitted its first black American student only seven years earlier, in September 1952. The Admissions Director, Headmaster and Trustees of the school had become interested in adding some diversity to the white, upper-middle-class student body by providing scholarships to a few well-qualified boys from abroad who could cope with the demanding curriculum. According to Lawrence M. Noble, the Admissions Director, in the fall of 1958 Groton School was contemplating "the desirability of taking an Oriental boy through the A[merican] F[ield] S[ervice], and of continuing our American Negro program." But in a prefatory note to a memo he submitted to the Reverend John Crocker, who was then in his eighteenth year as Headmaster, Noble recommended exploring with the Trustees "the possibility of taking a boy from Ghana next year" for several reasons: "the growing importance of Africa in the world picture, the leading position of Ghana in Africa, and its natural link with the U.S. through Prime Minister Nkrumah, and the special contact we have with the African American Institute, through our graduate, Alan Pifer, who will be in Ghana this fall."

The memo Noble attached provided detailed background information to support his recommendation:

We have received, during the past year and a half, letters from some fifteen Ghana boys expressing their desire to secure a scholarship for Groton. The first boy, Edward Butler, wrote in February, 1957. I replied that we could not consider him for that year, but might for the following year. His answer showed a strong desire to apply for 1958, "so that one day I will take part in building our new nation Ghana." I sent him a catalogue and application blank. Other boys, some of whom were friends of Butler, began writing me last summer and fall, and soon there were ten applicants. After discussing the whole matter with the Headmaster and Entrance Committee, including the difficulty of securing adequate information about these boys, as well as the financial problems and vacations, etc., the decision was reached to postpone consideration of the candidates to the following year. I wrote all the boys to this effect last November.

After considerable correspondence with the U.S. Information Service in Ghana, the Ghana Ministry of Education, the Headmaster of the Accra High School, and the African-American Institute, the following developments have taken place:

1. Mr. David Stratmon, Cultural Affairs Officer of the U.S. Information Service in Accra, has offered to do "all he can to assist in this most worthy project."
2. Mr. E. Jefferson Murphy, Director of the African Office of the African-American Institute, wrote last March that he will be glad to help us find a suitable boy.
3. Mr. John B. George of the African-American Institute wrote in May that "At the last meeting of the Board of Trustees the possibility of our granting an amount to provide his transportation to and from the United States and some monies during the vacation period was favorably considered."
4. Mr. W.F. Conton, Headmaster of the Accra High School, has been most cooperative in offering to assist, and in advising us about the Ghana schools and educational system.
5. Alan Pifer, '40, as you know from my memorandum to you of last June, is with the Carnegie Institute and is a Trustee of the African-American Institute. He is most interested in this project and will be in Ghana this fall. He could interview the candidates in person.

We should consider carefully the facts that in selecting a boy from Ghana, we would have not only the cooperation and assistance of the Ministry of Education and the African-American Institute, but the latter organization would finance the boy's transportation and vacations, and Alan Pifer would be able to interview the candidates personally. If we select a boy who has completed the Higher School Certificate, he would be adequately prepared for our Sixth Form course, and would presumably not have the language barrier...

I, personally, would favor our exploring further this project through the people mentioned above, and accepting a boy from Ghana if a really promising one can be found. The fact that fifteen boys from Ghana have, of their own accord, written and applied for admission to Groton does, it seems to me, present us with a unique opportunity to take the lead again in our admissions policy in a new field. These boys want an American education in order to serve their new free country. Among these fifteen boys there are probably several who will eventually be leaders and will play a part in the future relationship between the United States and the nations of Africa. However, this would mean adding another full scholarship to our budget, and I shall understand it if for financial or other reasons you and the Trustees should decide against it.

On the strength of this report, Noble was given permission to go ahead with the recruitment of a "Ghana boy." He immediately contacted Alan Pifer, the Groton graduate who had earlier expressed a willingness to assist his old school in this worthwhile project. Pifer recalls his involvement in the scheme as follows:

1. Knowing that I was interested in Africa and made frequent trips there, Groton School asked for my help in recruiting a suitable African student to spend a year at the School.
2. I agreed and as a trustee of the African-American Institute I sought its assistance in finding such a student.
3. More specifically, as I was soon to make a trip to Ghana I sought help from E. Jefferson (Pat) Murphy who was in charge of the AAI office in Accra.

4. Pat knew George [Ayi Kwei] Armah and knew he wanted to study in the U.S. Although George was already a graduate of Achimota School, Pat thought he would benefit from a year at a good American secondary school and therefore arranged for me to interview him when I got to Accra.
5. I did this, was favorably impressed and recommended him to Groton, which subsequently admitted George and gave him a full scholarship.
6. George liked Groton and Groton liked him. His year there was a considerable success both socially and academically. Having done 6th Form work at Achimota he was exceptionally well prepared.

But this may not be the whole story of how Armah got to Groton. A former teacher of his at Achimota, Adrian Sherwood, in a recent letter to James Gibbs, recalled the matter this way:

You wonder how the Groton offer to George Armah arose. I must have known but cannot exactly remember...It must have been soon after Vice-President Nixon's visit to Ghana (I think he came to represent the U.S.A. at the Independence celebrations, but that needs to be checked. He had just made the famously sickening speech on television with his wretched dog.) He came to address the School and made the most comical nonsense of it, giving us a post-graduate scholarship intended for [the University of Ghana at] Legon, which he was to visit in the afternoon. (This resulted in [a] junior Housemaster [getting launched on a] career as a biologist!). Whether Armah's scholarship was merely an expression of good will from America to the newly independent Ghana or an attempt to undo Nixon's gaffe I have no idea, but it would be interesting to find out.

Interesting indeed! Nixon did represent the United States at Ghana's independence celebrations on 6 March 1957, and during that visit he did speak at both Achimota and the University of Ghana. Although the documents from the Admissions Office at Groton show that one Achimota student, Edward Butler, had written as early as February 1957 asking for admission and scholarship assistance, they also show that some friends of Butler had sent similar letters during the summer and fall of 1957, following Nixon's visit. So there is at least a possibility that Armah's application and subsequent admission to a top American prep school was to some extent a consequence of Vice-President Nixon's magnanimous blunder when addressing students at Achimota. How ironic it would be if it turned out that Armah owed his education in America to a stupid mistake by Richard Nixon!

From Armah's application for admission to Groton School.

Armah unquestionably merited consideration for a scholarship at Groton. He had been one of Achimota's most outstanding students, regularly winning school prizes, earning a first-grade Cambridge School Certificate in 1956 with distinctions in English Language, English Literature, Geography, Latin and Science, and credits in French, History and Mathematics, and attaining a West African Higher School Certificate in 1958 after taking Form VI prizes in English, Geography and Latin. In addition he had been extremely active in extracurricular activities, especially sports (cricket, field hockey, soccer, swimming, table tennis, tennis, volleyball), drama, and school publications. In his final years at Achimota he had served as a writer and director of house and school plays, as editor of a house newspaper, as secretary of the School Prefectorial Council, and as editor and then editor-in-chief of the school magazine. He had also taken on various student administrative responsibilities: house librarian, house monitor, house representative to the school library committee, and house prefect. In short, he had been a conspicuous leader at Ghana's leading secondary school.

And his brilliance and versatility were immediately recognized by his teachers and fellow students at Groton. Taking courses in English, History, French, Latin, Latin Tutorial, and Sacred Studies, he quickly emerged as the best student in his class and graduated magna cum laude. Sherwood reports that he surprised Groton "by coming top in English in the Sixth Form," and he appears to have astonished his classmates in other ways too; the 1960 Groton School yearbook records that "Sixth Form year began with a rush of strange and new experiences from which we only partially recovered. These experiences were spiced with the arrival of Armah from Ghana, who shattered the rigid thought structures of nearly everyone who entered into conversation with him" (7).

He also gained a reputation as an "excellent passing and attacking" left wing for the Groton School soccer team (18); the yearbook notes that in one tight match "in the overtimes, there was no progress by either side until, with five seconds to play, Captain Bates poked in the ball that had come to him from Armah's corner kick" (18).

Armah taking a corner kick.

As at Achimota, Armah became an active member of the editorial board of the school literary magazine, *The Grotonian*. In the course of the 1959-60 academic year he contributed three articles to *The Grotonian*, and it is to these that we shall now turn our attention.

But first a word about his schoolboy writings at Achimota, where in 1958 and 1959 he did his share to fill up the pages of the school annual, *The Achimotan* (Lindfors). These early jottings included editorials, miscellaneous "School Notes," a three-and-a-half page mock epic poem, a house prefect's report, and a couple of humorous essays on topics of interest to schoolboys: mainly food, fads, false appearances, and schoolgirls. Achimota, unlike Groton in those days, was coeducational, and many of Armah's contributions to *The Achimotan* were lighthearted ruminations on some of the absurdities arising from the awkwardness of boy-girl relationships. He was especially adroit at teasing the girls for their "natural feminine diffidence," their giggling in the dining hall, and their heedless insensitivity to the pangs of adolescent love. But these sallies were not sharply satirical assaults on the opposite sex; they were bemused observations meant to tickle rather than to trash. Armah was writing as a campus wit, and girls were only one of his favorite soft targets. His was an innocent, almost gallant sort of sexist humor.

At Groton the contributions he made to the campus literary magazine were entirely different in nature and tone. Gone was the lightheartedness, the joking, the teasing, the relaxed frivolity. Gone too were the girls. Instead of aiming to entertain his classmates, Armah sought to instruct them about the wider world. His first essay was on Ghana, his second on Africa's present and future political alignments, and his third on the possible consequences of the Cold War struggle between the West and the East. Each essay in turn covered a broader span of the world's political geography, beginning with observations on Ghana's independence, then moving on to pan-African issues, and finally tackling global problems. He was exploring an ever-expanding universe of contemporary concerns, engaging in sober political analysis, not merely amusing himself and others with verbal hijinks. He was becoming a much more serious writer.

The essay on Ghana opened with a few basic facts about the geography and history of Africa before homing in on the Gold Coast and showing how British commercial activity there led to the imposition of colonial rule and to the concomitant restiveness of those being ruled. But the dissatisfied masses needed a leader. Armah's description of the emergence of Kwame Nkrumah is particularly interesting because it sounds at first very much like a praise song:

> Kwame Nkrumah was typical of Ghanaian youth in his dogged pursuit of learning. From a Catholic school in the western section of the colony, he went east to Achimota, a government-run Secondary School. Then, with considerable difficulty, he travelled to America where he studied in Lincoln and Pennsylvania

Universities. Nkrumah was always particularly aware of the injustice of imperial politics. In 1947, after a brief period in London, where he attended Communist meetings ("I just wanted to learn their organizational methods"), he arrived in the Gold Coast with a burning desire to liberate his countrymen, and with the supreme advantage of the would-be political revolutionary leader—he was completely impecunious. The head had joined the body.

Nkrumah swept through the whole country like some kind of tropical fever. Wherever he went, he spread the simple message: "Freedom." Soon every man, woman and child in the small British colony knew the name of Nkrumah. News of his exploits in his struggle against the wicked white man, relayed from town to village to remotest hut, and undergoing considerable change in the process, made him a living legend scarcely inferior to any of the numerous gods of tribal Paganism; and soon people who knew scarcely any other words of English were shouting, with various tribal accents, "FREEDOM, SELF GOV'MENT NOW!" (12-13)

But after independence "the old intertribal hostility reappeared" and "a species of civil war raged" so that "sharp measures were needed for the restoration of peace and order"(14):

Nkrumah adopted them. Declaring a state of emergency, he deported the most powerful troublemakers without trial, strengthened the police and army, and muzzled the opposition by putting its leaders behind bars.

These methods ultimately brought peace, but they also showed that Nkrumah had such a large majority in Parliament that he could establish a dictatorship at will. Such fears were strengthened when he proclaimed his birthday a national holiday, put his image on the country's coins and stamps, and generally assumed more and more power himself. (14)

This type of leadership led to further problems:

The most alarming manifestation of the government's new power is its apparent ability to disregard public opinion. With cynical disregard of what the people might think, the new administration displays now with uncouth ostentation such wealth as could not have been acquired honestly within such a short time. A situation has arisen in which bribery is the order of the day. (14)

Here in embryo is the situation described with so much venom in Armah's first novel, *The Beautyful Ones Are Not Yet Born*. The nationalist politician called "the new one" had initially inspired hope in the populace and had led them to independence but on attaining power had turned dictatorial and self-aggrandizing, thereby creating a climate of parasitic opportunism in which ostentatious government corruption, often manifested in the taking of bribes, became the order of the day. The public cynicism and "hope perennially doomed to disappointment" (14) that are so graphically depicted in this 1968 novel were being articulated by Armah in his November 1959 essay in *The Grotonian*, only two-and-a-half years after Ghana's independence. But back then Armah did manage to retain a shred of utopian optimism. He concluded his essay with a vision of pan-African unity, stating that "it is probable that in a decade or two Ghana will not be a separate country, but one of several states within a federal union of African nations" (15). Ironically, this had been Nkrumah's vision of the future of Africa, too.

Armah's next essay, "East, West, or Neuter?," in the February 1960 issue of *The Grotonian*, began with a quotation from Harold Macmillan's famous "Winds of Change" speech which envisioned the world as being divided into three great groups: the Western powers, the Eastern bloc of nations dominated by Communist Russia and China, and the nonaligned nations of the Third World. In the very year when many African countries were slated to make the transition from colonial status to independence, Armah was asking in which of these three camps they would be likely to end up. His answer was that "it is to the third group that the new African nations, at least for the time being, will orient themselves" (71). For one thing, the colonial record will go very heavily against the Western world. In the experimental years following independence, it will be eminently expedient to blame all teething troubles somehow on the white man. Such attitudes will always have at least a modicum of justification. (71)

Western imperialism, after all, "for the sake of commercial gain...destroyed the African's land, his secure tribal life, and, even more ruthlessly, his self-respect" (71). To prove that this "all-pervading, aggressive greed" (71) of Westerners was deliberately exploitative, Armah quoted an Anglocentric statement by Cecil Rhodes, lifting it from Lenin's book, *Imperialism, the Highest State of Capitalism*. Since it is unlikely that Armah would have been reading such a book for any of his courses at Groton, it is clear that even at the age of twenty Armah had already embarked on a program of self-education that went well beyond school textbooks. He was trying to come to terms with the dynamics of the West's intervention in Africa.

Africans, he said, were well aware of the prevalence of racism in the West, particularly in America and South Africa, but nonetheless,

> America, the most important of the Western galaxies, has not drawn upon herself any of the opprobrium attaching to the colonial countries. Thanks to the genial *bonhomie* of World War II GIs stationed in Africa and to the Hollywood western, America, or more correctly, Americans, enjoy an almost idolatrous popularity. In places the word Yankee, fraught with such unfortunate connotations in its own country, has come to mean not only everything American, but also everybody and everything which is beautiful, handsome, vivacious and 'progressive.' (72-73)

These positive opinions may have been shared by many Ghanaians who had never been to the United States; in his letter to James Gibbs, Adrian Sherwood remarked that "Ghana at the time was going through an uncritical pro-American phase." But for Armah the idolatry didn't last, as his novels *Fragments* and *Why Are We So Blest?* eloquently attest.

Communism, on the other hand, held certain attractions for Africans, according to the young Armah; in his essay he pointed to Russia's reputation for harmonious race relations as well as its rapid economic and scientific progress. It had "achieved the rags-to-riches dream" (73) and had also produced Sputniks. Moreover, it valued communalism and a more equitable distribution of wealth than any capitalistic society did. But even so, the influence of Russia was not very great in Africa, due in part to the banning of Communist organizations in European colonies.

Armah acknowledged the danger that African nations, even after independence, might continue to be "dominated from abroad through economic means" (74) and might become pawns in an international game of chess between East and West. Here he quoted Julius Nyerere's views on politically motivated foreign aid schemes that were meant to enlist the recipient on the side of the donor; again Armah's extracurricular reading had provided him with relevant food for thought, sharpening his own ideas on nonalignment.

He concluded his essay by repeating his vision of a "projected Union of Africa" (75) that would enable the continent to avoid divisive Balkanization. And he recommended that Africa in the meantime should keep its options open.

> The experience of older governments will be helpful, but Africans will most probably find no earthly reason for restricting themselves to this or that system, since no country or bloc claims a monopoly of either virtue or vice, incompetence or efficiency. Africans recognize a goal of sorts in their own future. The method of propulsion thither is likely to depend neither on comfort nor on sentiment. It will depend on speed. (75)

Armah's final essay, in the May 1960 issue of *The Grotonian*, was entitled "Cold Thaw—Deep Freeze" and drew on so many sources that he appended footnotes to the text. Among the works cited were Edward Chrankshaw's *Khrushchev's Russia*, Nikita Khrushchev's *For Victory in Peaceful Competition with Capitalism*, Gerald Clark's *Impatient Giant—Red China Today*, Harrison Salisbury's *To Moscow and Beyond*, and a jingoistic political article by Frank Meyer in the *National Review*. Since all these works were published in 1959 or 1960, Armah evidently was busy absorbing the very latest ideas on the Cold War. His essay appears to have been prompted in part by the upcoming Summit conference between Eisenhower and Khrushchev.

Armah first remarked on the "spirit of cautious, suspended optimism" (130) generated by the conference, a mood spoiled only by the looming threat now posed by China's growing power, which could involve the West "in a Cold War much more vicious than the first and infinitely more likely to turn hot" (130). Armah wanted "to try and understand the different phobias, complexes and aspirations that started and sustained the Cold War (and are going to do so again) *as the enemy sees them*" (131). He attributed "much of the blustering aggression and the self-righteous arrogance" of the Russians to "two collective complexes: those of inferiority and persecution" (131). The Soviet Union, "born amid great violence" (131) and seen as a threat by other governments, had been attacked by fourteen different states, a fact that had earned Russians the right to self-pity.

As for the Chinese, they

> share very closely Russia's collective complexes. They accuse the West of displaying a "superiority complex" and are extremely sensitive to the fact that for over a century their huge country was an inert mass on which marauding warlords, both foreign and indigenous, wrought their wanton wills. (132-133)

The Chinese had also suffered injustice, intimidation and persecution from enemies near and far, so they had strenuously sought to instill patriotism and pride in their people and to win recognition abroad for their remarkable economic progress which had been achieved through sheer hard work and a reverent subservience to Confucian teachings. America's failure to establish normal relations with a nation as powerful and potentially destructive as China was thus a colossal miscalculation. If an ability to negotiate with China ultimately led to an atomic war, "we shall all be in for another Ice Age" (134).

It appears unlikely that Armah would have been drawn to writing an essay of this sort had he remained in Ghana. His first year in America had provided him with much more than just another year of elite schooling; it had also furnished him with a broader perspective on human affairs, exposing him to currents of thought in circulation in a larger international arena. He no doubt had done a lot of this learning on his own, outside the classroom, but Groton had given him the opportunity to grow in ways that he himself had probably never anticipated. In the course of the year he had been converted from a "Ghana boy" to a young man of the world.

And not everything he had absorbed at that stage in his life had been learnt at school. Adrian Sherwood reported that while at Groton Armah

> made a close friend who had millionaire parents with a country estate. They were liberal enough to have George to stay in the holidays, but took the boys on trips abroad..., including [one to] Spain, where I understand that George was so upset by the contrast [between the luxury of the tourists' life and the poverty around him] that when the family offered to put him through Harvard, he refused...and worked his way through university by himself.

Well, maybe not entirely by himself. Harvard after all did award him an Honorary National Scholarship (a "full scholarship," according to Alan Pifer), so he may not have faced great financial hardship while studying there. Indeed, Armah himself has recalled some of his experiences at Groton and Harvard with great fondness, saying his American friends were "excellent [hosts]":

From my first minute in America I'd been treated courteously and kindly, and persons who were by any reckoning part of that country's power elite had made me a welcome friend in their homes. If anyone is qualified to speak of having lived through an idyllic spell of youth, I am. (1985: 1752)

That charmed youth appears to have ended before he left Harvard in 1963, but his first academic year in the United States, the Groton year, may have been his very best and by far his most idyllic.

Sixth Form

Rear Row: S. Cobb, Robbins, Sloan, Randolph, N. Pierce, Richards.
Third Row: Choate, Bates, Offner, Slocum, Elliston, Pollock, Gund, Temple.
Second Row: Nitze, P. Edwards, Percival, Cochran, von Blanckensee, Purtell, Hare, Spofford, Richdale, L. Thorne, Chace.
Front Row: Tong, Armah, Rand, F. Kellogg, Bingham, Keyes (*Secretary*), Hallowell, P. Magowan, Crosby, Gaver, Lloyd, Green.

Soccer Squad

Rear Row: Mr. Smith, Mr. Sackett, Lee (*Manager*), Mr. Nichols.
Middle Row: Hadley, Krech, Patterson, Temple, Offner, R. Whitney, Sloan, S. Cheever, Butler, Lloyd, J. Bordley.
Front Row: Randolph, Edwards, D. Thorne, R. Knapp, Nitze, Cochran, Bates (*Captain*), Armah, Richdale, Auchincloss, McBaine, Brooks.
Missing: J. Whitman.

Armah's Harvard Writings

In an autobiographical essay entitled "One Writer's Education" Ayi Kwei Armah sought to set the record straight about his academic career. Two literary critics had erroneously reported that he had "spent several years in America as a high school student and an undergrad at Harvard, graduating with a B.A. *summa cum laude* in Sociology" (Armah 1752). According to Armah, the truth of the matter was that

> After completing my secondary and sixth form education at Achimota, then working for eight months as a Radio Ghana scriptwriter, reporter and announcer, I left for America as a scholarship student. I spent precisely one academic year (September 1959 to June 1960) at Groton, the Massachusetts prep school, before taking the various exams and entering Harvard. Since there is a false but widely advertised impression that I was practically a baby when I left Ghana to study in America, I should perhaps point out that I was already 19 years old, and had experienced life as an independent working adult in Accra, when I left for America.
>
> I entered Harvard University in September 1960 and left in Spring 1963, my final year, without waiting to finish my courses and examinations. However fine my course grades, there was no way I could have got a *summa* under those circumstances. More to the point, by my final undergraduate year such matters as academic kudos, social status and professional careers had already come to seem profoundly irrelevant to me...
>
> I left Harvard before the official end of my undergraduate studies because concurrently with my academic work I'd been trying to decide what my lifework was to be...

When I entered Harvard in 1960, it was my intention to specialise in Literature. In my first year, however, my centre of interest shifted from the contemplation of arrangements of symbols, images and words, to a scrutiny of the arrangements of the social realities buried under those words, images and symbols...

I had precise ideas about what I needed to study. But at first I could find no single department at the university offering the full range of interdisciplinary courses I was determined to take. Persistent investigation revealed there was indeed a likely programme, but it was a pilot programme not yet advertised in the academic catalogue. Admission was restricted to Social Science students meeting specific academic standards. I registered for the requisite courses, met the stipulated standards and got into the experimental Social Studies programme.

It was just what I'd been searching for. It opened up the various Social Science disciplines in such a way that the interconnections between the economics of continents, the politics of nations and the sociology and culture of peoples were made systematically clear.

The consummation of this new love did not mean an abandonment of Literature. But there too my interest shifted significantly, from appreciation to production, from literary theology to creative and expository writing as craft and art.

Something else happened. My old respect and affection for authors whose work had moved me was now transferred, not indeed to eminent sociologists, but to persons and groups that had worked to create new, better social realities in place of those they had found at birth. These, after all, were practically involved in creativity of a more difficult and necessary type, and it mattered not at all that their work was essentially anonymous. It was to that kind of creativity that I wanted to engage my life. (1752-53)

Upon leaving Harvard Armah went to Mexico and then to Algeria, where he worked for less than a year[1] as a translator for the English edition of a magazine called *Revolution Africaine*. During this period his health broke down, "destroyed by months of malnourishment, poor accommodation and sheer uncertainty," and for the first time in his life he was "ill enough to be hospitalised, first in Algiers, then in Boston. It's an understatement to say I had a nervous breakdown: it was my entire being, body and soul, that had broken down" (1753). After five months of rehabilitation he returned to Ghana and started writing novels.

His years at Harvard, where he had broadened the scope of his reading, honed the "craft and art" of his writing, and defined a long-term goal for himself, could thus be said to have changed the course of his life, leading him to look for work that he felt would help to make the world a better place, work that was both creative and politically committed. "By the beginning of my final year," he said, "I had decided, if possible, to work with the liberation movements in southern Africa, all involved, from my perspective, in the same fundamental process" (1752). So eager was he to pursue some semblance of this ambition that he was prepared to drop out of Harvard just before graduation and join the ill-paid staff of an anti-imperial magazine in Algiers. And there it may have been more than just his physical health that broke down. As his novel *Why Are We So Blest?* shows, he became disillusioned with the north African revolutionary movement itself, and this may have been one of the factors contributing to his "nervous breakdown," which appears to have been a collapse of mind as well as of "body and soul." What Armah does not mention in his account of his student years is that he did go on to complete his Harvard course work in 1964, presumably while convalescing at a Boston hospital. He left the United States with his B.A. degree in hand.

From the 1960 Groton School Yearbook

GEORGE ARYEE-QUAYE
ARMAH
49 Elm St., Wellesley, Mass.
Groton School
English

From the Harvard freshman Register for the class of 1964.

The writing Armah did at Harvard is therefore of considerable interest because one may assume that it reflects some of his leading preoccupations and concerns during this pivotal phase in his life. There are four pieces worth examining: his B.A. thesis on "The Romantic Response to the Industrial Revolution: A Sociological Study of the Works of William Blake (1757-1827) and William Wordsworth (1770-1850)" submitted on 29 March 1963 by Ai Kwei Armah; a short story entitled "The Ball" published in the *Harvard Advocate* in 1964 by George A.K. Armah; a short story entitled "The Offal Kind" by Aryeequaye Armah that won *Drum*'s 1963 Pan-African Short Story Contest and was published in the January 1964 issue of *Drum* and reprinted with only minor revisions five years later in *Harper's Magazine*, after his first novel *The Beautyful Ones Are Not Yet Born* (1968) had captured the world's attention; and an essay on "Pan-Africanism and the White Man's Burden" published in the *Harvard Journal of Negro Affairs* in 1965 by Aryee Quaye Armah. It may have been "The Ball" or "The Offal Kind" that earned Armah a Harvard prize for best short fiction in 1963 (Ezugu i).

Armah's 86-page B.A. thesis is an impressive piece of work written with more fluency and authority than most undergraduate academic theses ordinarily exhibit. It begins with a 15-page chapter succinctly summarizing "The Industrial Revolution in Britain: Some Relevant Aspects," goes on to recount the life histories of Wordsworth and Blake, and then discusses the impact of the industrial revolution on their poetry, demonstrating that Romanticism as an art form arose as a response to the process of rapid modernization in Britain. There is nothing startlingly new in this argument on the Romantic impulse in British poetry, but Armah builds his case effectively by relying on recognized authorities for historical and biographical information and by offering his own insightful analyses of passages from relevant texts by Wordsworth and Blake.

Throughout the thesis Armah displays an ability to think for himself, unfettered by some of the scholarship he cites. Indeed, at times he is quite amusing when expressing ironic skepticism about some of the claims advanced by sycophantic pedants. For instance, on the subject of Wordsworth's marriage to his well-to-do cousin and schoolmate Mary Hutchinson, Armah states that

> Sutherland, whose biography is designed to present the poet as a fine, upstanding, monogamous paragon of social virtue, goes to no small amount of trouble to describe the affection and warmth which he supposed to have existed between man and wife. Only as an afterthought does he throw out the statement: "Mrs. Wordsworth, it may be added, was not without fortune." (18)

Here and elsewhere Armah proves capable of reading between the lines of the available biographical record and forming his own impressions of Wordsworth. On another occasion he puts forward the opinion that "It might sound like an evil thing to say, but it seems clear that the great freedom enjoyed by the poet in his childhood would not have been possible without the opportune demise of his parents" (25).

Armah portrays Wordsworth as an individual devoted to leisure and self-indulgence, someone totally out of touch with the workaday world who

> made no attempt to fit himself for a life of anything other than contemplation. Not that he did not see the importance of "gainful employment." On the contrary, he seems to have found it praiseworthy in peasants and other lower class people that they should be engaged in such employment. The truth seems to be that Wordsworth thought the injunction "In the sweat of thy brow shalt thou eat bread," applicable only to the lower elements of society, who otherwise would have been drawn unresisting into mischief. (33)

Given Armah's ardent proletarian sympathies, expressed not long afterwards in his story "The Offal Kind" as well as in his first novel *The Beautyful Ones Are Not Yet Born*, it is not at all surprising that he disdains Wordsworth's snooty slothfulness and unwillingness to work and sweat alongside "the lower elements of society." Armah recognizes this iconoclastic streak in his own attitude toward Wordsworth, but he has little patience with the poet's ingrained class-consciousness and weak-willed waffling on important social and moral issues. He concedes that

> The question of Wordsworth's personal integrity is a touchy one. The morality of those to whom society vouchsafes a place in the pantheon of heroes is generally regarded as a field beyond inquiry. Yet dig we must. There is much reason to think Wordsworth made it his primary concern in life to defend himself from life. He was intolerant of worrisome concerns, and preferred peace to conviction. He seems to have found it easy enough to hold noble opinions, until events challenged his good faith. (33-34)

The poet's initial enthusiasm and later disillusionment with the French Revolution serves as a case in point.

> Like many a deserter from a good cause, Wordsworth was not tardy in finding reasons for believing that he had not betrayed his cause, but that, forsaking the path of virtue, it had betrayed him....At the bottom of such convictions there must have been a profound unwillingness, even an inability, to come to a sympathetic understanding of the oppressed. For all his talk of peasant virtue, Wordsworth does not seem to have had any really intimate contact with the lowly. Not a few of his poems on the lower classes were embellishments of second-hand stories. (35-36)

Armah concludes by asserting that Wordsworth's counter-revolutionary tendencies, prompted by his inability to adhere to any fixed moral code that made demands on his tranquillity, betrayed a

> personality, whose cardinal quality is the desire not to create or be involved with any disturbance: the desire for peace and quiet. Anything requiring great energy and powers of organization was

likely to strike into Wordsworth a baffled helplessness. He was, by both nature and training, a conservative. (37)

Armah, by this time a romantic revolutionary himself, could not find anything to admire in such aloofness, such helplessness, such nonchalant and feckless imperturbability.

In the next chapter of his thesis Armah finds himself equally unimpressed with Blake, but for different reasons. Blake had bonafide credentials as a free-thinking, lower-class radical, but his ideas about art and about the singularity of his own god-given creative powers limited what he was able to achieve both as a graphic artist and as a poet. His major fault, according to Armah, was his lack of discipline:

> Training in Art seemed to Blake an unnecessarily restrictive process, likely to vitiate the truth of creative vision with acquired affectation; to the adamantine stubbornness with which he stuck to this view of the necessity for spontaneity we owe the imperfections of technique in both his art and his poetry. He sincerely believed himself to be operating under some divine inspiration, and would have been inclined to dismiss as mere impertinence those of his critics who wondered if his deitie[s] were ignorant of the rules of scansion and spelling. (42)

Armah feels that Blake in his own way was as much an elitist as Wordsworth, the difference being that Blake believed himself to be endowed with truly visionary gifts:

> Blake throughout his life continued to regard himself as a sort of prophet, a poet with a duty to communicate his powerful spontaneous visions to the rest of mankind. It is hard to escape the impression that he regarded himself as some higher sort of human being, and thought it would be to the good of other men if they would allow themselves to aspire to the level of his own powers of perception, and even beyond. (43)

Again it is the egotism of the artist who prides himself on being superior to others in wisdom, insight, feeling and gentility that attracts Armah's scorn.

This is particularly interesting given the privileged place occupied by unusually gifted "seers" in Armah's later fiction, especially *Two Thousand Seasons* (1973), *The Healers* (1978), and *Osiris Rising* (1995). Armah's deep thinkers, however, are highly disciplined, politically committed revolutionaries who fight on the side of the oppressed. They are supremely intelligent and creative beings, but they do not position themselves above their society looking down. Instead, rather like the young Armah leaving Harvard, they become "practically involved in creativity of a more difficult and necessary type" and work "to create new, better social realities in place of those they found at birth" (1753). Their high-minded idealism and plebeian sympathies mark them as Romantic conceptions, but they have their feet grounded firmly in the mire in ways that Wordsworth and Blake did not. Armah's research for his B.A. thesis may have helped him to clarify his ideas on what his lifework should be, moving him away from effete elitism toward creatively constructive forms of social engagement.

Armah's short stories, "The Ball" and "The Offal Kind," are remarkable for the sympathy they express for young people whose lives are made miserable by cruel, domineering elders in positions of authority over them. "The Ball" has as its central character a middle-class boy who, like Armah himself, is the son of respectable schoolteachers. Unlike other boys and girls his age, "children from bad broken homes" (36), Kwame is not allowed to play gutterball in the busy streets of his town or to get his clothes wet by running and sliding in the rain or to throw stones at clusters of ripe mangoes, knocking them down from the trees, or to frolic in the surf and sand of the beach.

> He at least had a mother to control him, marching straight to school and back every day, doing what he was told, getting good marks and being the first boy in the class...But he could only look with

childish wonder and deep longing, envious longing, and if this longing threatened to break out into action he only had to remember his mother's apprehensive words, remember how all these children, improperly happy, had come from bad broken homes. With that the tight controlled being within him would take over, and he would move on, thinking of bad broken homes and the happiness of the children playing in the street. (35 36)

Kwame's father had died years before, and his mother was intent on sending her only son to study in England so he could "become a great respected man some day, greater even than his father" (38), possibly even an engineer earning a hundred pounds a month. So Kwame had to follow a straight and narrow academic path, forgoing all the innocent pleasures of youth.

But one day he yields to temptation. While helping the servant girl Adjoa carry his mother's bundles, he falls into conversation with a man walking along beside them. The man, on learning that Kwame enjoys playing soccer, offers to give him a ball, saying Kwame will have to fetch it from a woman seated some distance up the road. Kwame runs off to the woman only to discover that she knows nothing about the ball or about the man who sent him to collect it. The boy realizes he has been tricked. When he gets back to Adjoa, he finds that his mother's two bundles have been stolen from her by the man who had duped him.

> Later at school his mother shed tears as she told his teacher what the boy had done. She pleaded with the teacher to drive the lesson in so hard he would never forget it. Never trust a stranger. With shame in his breast the teacher complied with the mother's wishes. Even before the first stroke the boy was hollering, asking both mother and teacher to understand and to spare him. But they did not hear his begging. (40)

Kwame thereafter resumes his rigid routine, marching straight to school and back every day, never joining his agemates in any games, but still enviously watching "the others at play, the balls shooting back and forth, the children swiftly, skilfully careening down the gutters, dodging the big waves on the seashore" (40). Like a junior version of "the man" in *The Beautyful Ones Are Not Yet Born*, Kwame appears to have nothing left to look forward to in life. And like Baako in *Fragments* he finds himself at odds with the materialistic values of an older generation. But unlike either of these adult heroes, he is too young to chart an independent course for himself so he plods on obedient to the dictates of his harsh, controlling mother. He is an unhappy victim of her quest for social standing and upward mobility.

In "The Offal Kind" the crushed adolescent protagonist is a young girl who is driven into prostitution by the predatory cruelties of an older woman. Araba's mother sends her away at a young age to be a lady's domestic servant, where "if she was good and learned everything there was to learn, she would perhaps be a lady herself one day, perhaps" (35; 79). The lady works her hard and feeds her little, and when Araba tries to improve her lot be selling tiger nuts at night at a bus stop, the lady rebukes her, calling her a thief and a wastrel. But subsequently the lady decides to put the girl to work as a petty trader selling biscuits and cigarettes to fishermen, a job that is profitable in the dry season but much more difficult when the rains begin.

One day Araba is tricked out of all her goods by a group of boys, and the lady beats her severely and feeds her even less. To alleviate her hunger pangs, she starts haggling for food whenever she is sent on errands to the market. When the lady finds out, she chases Araba out of her house, telling her never to come back. The girl sleeps that night in a lorry park until woken up by a policewoman who takes her to a Remand Home where she is incarcerated for vagrancy. She escapes, meets a young truck driver, and spends the night with him. The next morning he leaves her with a kindly old woman who runs a brothel where she is treated very well. The old woman encourages her to go back to the Remand Home and serve out her sentence. Araba does so but returns to the brothel afterwards in order to begin work as a prostitute. She is too ashamed to go home to her village. She has been reduced to human rubbish, the offal kind.

Derek Wright, one of the few scholars to have commented on this story, makes the interesting observation that

> Armah has deliberately conceived this story after the pattern of Victorian England at the peak of its colonial power. From a rural family-system that can no longer take care of its children, girls are farmed out to self-styled aristocrats in whose employ they regress from household servants to the status of medieval serfs. Affecting a nineteenth-century remoteness from the masses, doubtless learned from the colonial cadres on which they model themselves, this Victorianized elite mentally reduces the abandoned of the city to the human refuse of the title. For those who work in this living museum of English Victorianism, there is nothing in life except work...Driven penniless from the house of the society-woman and into vagrancy, Araba is kept from returning to her family home by a Victorian sense of shame...The vagrant girls go round and round in an endless circle, serving the exploitative interests of an affluent Westernized elite which has carefully cultivated the legacy of Victorian imperialism in the post-Independence period. (23)

All this may be true, but in another sense "The Offal Kind," like "The Ball," is a story of the maiming of the young by the old, the vulnerable by the powerful, the child by the parent or by those who serve *in loco parentis*. This generational struggle in both stories may have less to do with colonialism and class than it does with betrayals of blood and kinship. Kwame's mother and Araba's employer are cruel, callous elders unbonded by love and respect to the youngsters closest to them. They have lost all sympathy, all compassion, for those who depend on them. Armah appears to be criticizing the sort of people whose yearnings for social position and personal comfort harden their hearts, turning them into monsters who mercilessly destroy their own kind. Such insensitive brutes have been not just Westernized or Victorianized but almost totally dehumanized. Like the rotting banister in *The*

Beautyful Ones Are Not Yet Born, they have been corrupted from within as well as soiled from without. They are socially and spiritually dead.

Armah's short stories are interesting as precursors of his longer fiction, for they deal with some of the same matters that loom large in his novels: blighted hopes and dreams, damaged human relationships, soul-destroying greed and materialism, exploitation and persecution of the weak by the strong, physical and psychological suffering, and pervasive despair. These were themes he returned to repeatedly in his more mature works. It is significant that he was already beginning to probe them as an undergraduate at Harvard.

Armah's essay on "Pan-Africanism and the White Man's Burden" likewise reflects what he thought at this point in his life about the effects of colonialism, nationalism and independence on Africa in general and on Ghana in particular. Indeed, the essay gives evidence of how "the interconnections between the economics of continents, the politics of nations and the sociology and culture of peoples were made systematically clear" to him through his immersion in Harvard's experimental Social Studies programme. Using Karl Mannheim's twin concepts of "ideology" and "utopia" to distinguish between the thinking of ruling groups and the thinking of those ruled, Armah posits that

> Pan-African utopianism is not merely a reaction, an opposition to the ideology of the White Man's Burden, but that the former is an outgrowth of the latter. An attempt will therefore be made to prove that the seeds of Pan-Africanism can be found in Britain's imperial ideology, and that it is through the working out of the ideology that Pan-Africanism came to fruition. (28)

To demonstrate this, Armah first examines conditions and in Britain and the Gold Coast in the closing decades of the nineteenth century, when European imperialism was at its height. The British, with a supreme self-confidence emanating from "an amalgam of Darwinism, Victorian Liberalism, Protestant

Christianity and patriotism" (29), fancied themselves biologically and morally superior to Africans, whom they regarded as backward, wicked children. Hence, the British felt they had a right, even a duty, to rule over such benighted creatures; this was the "white man's burden." Or as Armah mordantly puts it,

> the black and the white cried out for union. The African, full of vice, lost in the heathen darkness, needed light, civilization and Christianity. The Englishman, nigh choking with an excess of virtue and skill in government, brimming over with commercial prosperity and the grace of God, was in need of virgin fields wherein to exercise his plenitude of arts. Thus was ordained the meeting of black demand and white supply. (31)

But the success of this imperial conjunction eventually spelt its doom, for over time the ideology of the White Man's Burden produced a reaction amongst Africans that led to Pan-African self-assertion and revolution. Armah sees this as happening in four stages: 1. a period of impotence when the native intelligentsia had neither position nor power; 2. a period when African intellectuals such as Aggrey and Casely-Hayford claimed some attention for themselves but remained humble and compliant colonial subjects; 3. a period during which the intelligentsia, with the help of the old feudal elite and an emerging merchant class, began to assert itself, claiming a right to share in colonial government; 4. a period following the Second World War when nationalist politicians mobilized the masses and successfully challenged the fundamental tenets of British rule, including the notion that Africans were not on an equal footing with their erstwhile colonial masters. Armah then concludes by reiterating his thesis that Pan-Africanism is "the product of a dialectical process initiated by the imperial intrusion, the utopian outgrowth of the colonialist ideology" (40).

This is a cogent and cleverly constructed argument that draws its strength from Armah's methodical exploration of the history, politics, economics and psychology of the colonial era. Relying in equal measure upon sociological theory, cross-cultural comparison, and adroit analysis of conflicting statements made by Lord Lugard and Rudyard Kipling on the one hand and J.E. Casely-Hayford and Kwame Nkrumah on the other, he persuasively builds his case, occasionally underscoring his points with mocking sarcasm. He includes tidbits of information gleaned from the research he did for his B.A. thesis on the industrial revolution, but mostly he plows fresh ground, utilizing sources from a variety of disciplines. If we compare this essay with one Armah wrote on "Ghana" five years earlier at Groton School, we see a striking advance in his understanding of the dynamics of colonialism and in his handling of complex ideas. He was now a skilled social scientist as well as a graceful expository writer.

The writing Armah did at Harvard may yield insights into what was on his mind during this formative period in his life, but these few essays and sketches do not give us the full story of his intellectual growth and development during his undergraduate years. We still don't know why he suddenly dropped out of the university and ran off to Algeria via Mexico. For an explanation of that decision we need to return to his autobiographical essay, "One Writer's Education," written more than twenty years later. There Armah attributes his shift of focus from Literature to Social Studies as having been

accelerated by the events of the Congo crisis, culminating in the murder of Patrice Lumumba.

The assassination of Lumumba created in me the kind of deep-running sadness usually provoked by some irreplaceable personal loss. The reason is not really hard to find. I had long had a sense of myself not simply as an Akan, an Ewe, a Ghanaian and a West African, but most strongly and significantly as an African. It was as an African, then, that I contemplated, then understood, Lumumba's murder.

I used, then as now, to read both carefully and widely. I therefore knew Lumumba had worked to create a unified national movement in a fragmented land, had come to power through democratic elections, and, to judge by all he said, aspired to move together with all Africans from a servile to an independent, self-reliant status. When he was murdered even the most obtuse African student knew it was because the West, America in the lead, did not want to see potentially creative Africans in power.

In my general reading I had come to be suitably impressed by the consistency with which America and the West promoted parasitic, dictatorial regimes outside their own home grounds, supporting Chiang against Mao in China for instance, Diem against Ho in Vietnam, Somoza against Sandino in Nicaragua, Batista against Castro in Cuba. I kept relating this pattern of Western political preferences to developments at home in Africa, and, against the background of abundant historical evidence, the conclusion that presented itself to my mind was inexorable: if we Africans were to rise from the abyss of exploitation and contempt, we would be obliged to do so against murderous opposition from the West, America in the lead, the same way the Chinese, the Vietnamese, the Cubans had.

And yet my personal truth was that the Americans were my hosts, excellent ones at that. From my first minute in America I'd been treated courteously and kindly, and persons who were by any reckoning part of that country's power elite had made me a welcome friend in their homes. If anyone is qualified to speak of having lived through an idyllic spell of youth, I am.

Still, in my attempt to attain knowledge of the world in which I was to become a fully conscious adult, and perhaps to reach a clear understanding of my own probable function within that world, I was trying to balance the kindness, the respect and the abundant love bestowed on my individual person against the enormity of the crime committed against Lumumba, the Congo, Africa. In this attempt I felt initially hampered by the fact that I had not systematically studied the economic, social, political and, ultimately, philosophical and cultural issues at stake not only in the Congo but also in Angola, Azania, Zimbabwe, Namibia, in Africa as a whole and in the world at large. I wanted to end this state of relative ignorance. I decided to switch from Literature to Social Science. (1752-53)

The crisis in the Congo had started a few months before Armah had entered Harvard. The country had gained its independence on June 30, 1960, and had almost immediately been plunged into strife by a mutiny in the Congolese Army. On July 11th the province of Katanga seceded, and the Congolese government appealed first to the United States and then to the United Nations for military assistance. The U.N. quickly assembled a peacekeeping force made up mainly of units from various African states which were later supplemented by units from Europe and Asia. But since the U.N. contingent could act only in self-defense, it could not take the initiative in putting down the secession or in removing Belgian troops who had been sent in to protect Belgian nationals in the country. Patrice Lumumba, serving as Congolese Premier, appealed for support to Communist China, the Soviet Union, Ghana and other governments, setting up the possibility of an East-West confrontation over the region. On September 5th Congolese President Joseph Kasavubu dismissed Lumumba, and the situation deteriorated further, leading within a week to a military coup by Col. Joseph Mobutu. Five months later, on 13 February 1961, Lumumba, who had been transferred to Katanga under arrest, was killed, purportedly after escaping. Thereafter the Congo situation remained unstable until the U.N. command, moving against Katanga in force, ended the secession in January 1963, just a few months before Armah decided to leave Harvard.

Armah had spent the summer of 1960 working as a copy clerk for the *Washington Post*, where his duties included the collation and distribution of wirephoto and telenews copy as well as factotum work on the editorial floor (Ezugu iii). He therefore was in a good position to monitor the news coming from the Congo during that eventful summer. When he got to Harvard, the Congo crisis continued to feature prominently in the press, especially after the U.N. became involved in the conflict. The murder of Lumumba and the cold war struggle that preceded and ensued from it persuaded him that the United

States and other Western nations "did not want to see potentially creative Africans in power" (1752).

Toward the end of his senior year at Harvard there were some things happening within the United States that may have reinforced Armah's decision to depart. Bombs exploding at a motel for blacks and at the home of Dr. Martin Luther King, Jr. had led to riots and demonstrations in Birmingham. The mood there and in other black communities throughout the nation was so tense that President Kennedy had felt it necessary to warn Governor George Wallace that he was expected to ensure that an atmosphere of law and order prevailed in Alabama. Kennedy also took steps to arrange a 24-hour truce in Birmingham in exchange for promises by white leaders that the justifiable needs of black residents would be met. Meanwhile Attorney-General Robert F. Kennedy was filing a federal court order forbidding a Mississippi sheriff from using threats or violence to discourage the registration of black voters. In the early 1960s there was constant and continuing turmoil in America over civil rights, especially in the deep south.

At the same time that this struggle was going on, Armah was getting involved in a racial controversy at Harvard. Black students were seeking university approval of the formation of a "Harvard Association of African and Afro-American Students" that would restrict its membership to the fewer than one hundred Africans and Afro-Americans then enrolled at Harvard and its sister institution Radcliffe. However, the Harvard Council for Undergraduate Affairs (HCUA), which had preliminary jurisdiction in such matters, had reservations about recommending recognition of an organization that had a "discriminatory membership clause" that would exclude white students. According to the campus newspaper, *The Harvard Crimson*, Armah, as spokesman for the proposed "club," argued

> that the association had not defined itself in racial terms by using the phrase "African and Afro-American," and that the group's members considered race unimportant to their membership clause.

He objected to the word "Negro" as a description of the group's membership. He said the terms "African" and "Afro-American" covered many races, including Arabs and persons of partial European descent. In a later interview, he added that "Africans and Afro-Americans" included "people who are more white than black." Armah emphasized, however, that the group did not consider persons from colonial nations who resided in Africa as "Africans." (Rice 1)

It was also reported that during the two-hour debate on the issue

several HCUA members suggested to Armah that the association should have concealed its intentions for selecting members from its constitution. Armah replied: "We do not wish to sink to that moral level." (Rice 2)

When the vote finally was taken, the HCUA by a margin of 14-5-1 refused to recommend approval of the proposed association. This happened on May 6th, early in the three-week reading period preceding final examinations, which were due to start on May 22nd. For Armah, it may have been the last straw, for shortly thereafter he packed his bags and headed for Mexico.

Multiply disillusioned, Armah left Harvard and the United States only to face greater disillusionment and a devastating nervous breakdown in Algeria. But even after he started to recover, a problem remained:

how to work up some semblance of motivation for living in a world dying for change, but which I couldn't help to change. I knew I could write, but the question that immobilised me then remains to this day: of what creative use are skilfully arranged words when the really creative work—changing Africa's social realities for the better—remains inaccessible?

For I saw and still see the neo-colonial order we're all living with as profoundly destructive, its ruling arrangements incurably parasitic. That knowledge had long killed in me any desire to commit my life to any career in this old world masquerading as new....In the end, I waited till I felt marginally strong enough, then made the inescapable decision: I would revert to writing, not indeed as the most desired creative option, but as the least parasitic option open to me. When I returned to Ghana in 1964, there was nothing at home so unexpected as to shock me. Rather, I was in the position of a spore which, having finally accepted its destiny as a fungus, still wonders if it might produce penicillin. (1753)

Armah's years in the United States thus led him to choose a career for himself that might enable him to assist in the rehabilitation of Africa and thereby cure his own lingering malaise.

Harvard had put him in a fertile academic culture where his creative and socially constructive propensities could grow, develop and mature, but shortly before the end of his senior year he felt ripe and ready to enter the real world so he set out on an idealistic quest for self-fulfillment through self-sacrifice and revolutionary action. There he suffered a debilitating setback that forced him to reconsider his options in life. By the time he returned to Ghana, he had resolved to "revert to writing," hoping that "skilfully arranged words" would enable him to contribute to the moral and political reconstruction of modern Africa. He saw Africa as sick, and like the heroes in some of his novels, he wanted to serve as its healer, ridding it of colonial and neocolonial infections by injecting it with his own recuperative spirit, which would behave as a kind of prophylactic antibiotic, a life-saving penicillin. He had long thought of himself "not simply as an Akan, an Ewe, a Ghanaian and a West African but most strongly and significantly as an African," so he sought both to make Africa more conscious of its ills and to prescribe corrective remedies for what was wrong. It was by assuming this role as a diagnostic physician for the entire continent that Armah found a satisfying new direction for his own life, making it possible for him to begin the process of healing himself.

[1] He refers to this period in his life as lasting "nine months" (1753), but in his essay "Larsony" he records that he spent no more than seven months (June-December 1963) in Mexico and Algeria. (3)

Amos Tutuola, Oral Tradition, and the *Motif-Index*

Everybody talks about Amos Tutuola's debt to West African oral tradition but hardly anyone has done anything about it. A few critics have discussed a few folktales that have been woven into the loose fabric of Tutuola's long-winded yarns (Belvaude, Collins, Jones, Lindfors [1968-69, 1972], Obiechina), but no one has attempted a systematic survey of precisely how much material this eccentric Nigerian storyteller has borrowed, stolen or transformed from indigenous oral narratives. It was this sad scholarly gap in African literary folkloristics that I once aspired in some small measure to fill.

Since an adequate index of West African tale types did not exist,[1] I had to begin with the only research tools available: Stith Thompson's *Motif-Index of Folk-Literature* and Kenneth Clarke's "Motif-Index of the Folktales of Culture Area V, West Africa." Using Thompson's homespun rule-of-thumb definition of motif as "something out of the ordinary, something of sufficiently striking character to become a part of tradition, oral or literary" (19), I managed to extract 299 distinct motifs from the 119 pages of Tutuola's first and most famous book, *The Palm-Wine Drinkard and His Dead Palm-Wine Tapster in the Dead's Town.* It is perhaps worth noting that two hundred of these motifs fell into the following phantasmagoric categories: F. Marvels (81), D. Magic (54), B. Mythical Animals (44), G. Ogres (21).

Nearly fifty percent (143) of the total number of motifs were not listed in Thompson. Such a high percentage of new motifs suggested that *The Palm-Wine Drinkard* was an extremely original work, owing less to folklore than most observers supposed. This conclusion was supported by the fact that very few of these new motifs could be found in West African folktales; only 3 out of the 143 were listed in Clarke. A close look at the nature of these new motifs revealed that 61 out of the 143 (43%) were descriptive details relating to the appearance of persons or creatures, a fact which confirmed common sense suspicions that Tutuola's hyperbolic descriptions of men and monsters probably owed more to his imagination than to tradition. But the percentage of new motifs that were not purely descriptive details (57% of the new motifs; 28% of the total number of motifs) suggested that Tutuola was much more than simply an inventive portrait artist and that *The Palm-Wine Drinkard* was far more than a patchwork of borrowed materials. All the external evidence seemed to point to the conclusion that Tutuola was in most respects a highly original creative writer.

Of the 156 motifs from *The Palm-Wine Drinkard* that could be found listed in Thompson, slightly better than one-quarter (40) were listed in Clarke. To this number could be added the three motifs which were listed in Clarke but not in Thompson. In other words, out of a total of 299 motifs in *The Palm-Wine Drinkard* it was possible to prove that 43 (14.3%) were a part of West African oral tradition. This may seem like a small and insignificant number unless we keep certain facts in mind. First, folktale collecting in West Africa has been spotty and irregular (Bascom). Tales have been collected from most of the major ethnic and linguistic groups, but many groups are very poorly represented. A motif-index based on these collections is certain to omit a great part of West African oral tradition.

Secondly, a motif-index is an imperfect tool which is apt to make differences in degree appear to be differences in kind. A motif which is marked as "not listed in Thompson and Clarke" may in fact be closely related to several motifs that are listed in these works. But even the most painstaking cross-references will not make these relationships completely clear. As a result, many motifs listed as "new" may be only variants of very old, very popular narrative ideas. When working with such an unreliable tool, statistics may be misleading.

Thirdly, when motifs from *The Palm-Wine Drinkard* can be found listed in Clarke, they often prove to have a high frequency and wide distribution in West Africa (see, for example, F 611.3.2 and K 735.). Thus we can be fairly certain that Tutuola has borrowed these motifs from West African oral tradition. But until more tales are collected in West Africa and their motifs indexed, we cannot be certain that the remaining 256 motifs have not been borrowed or derived from West African oral tradition.

Finally and perhaps most importantly, motif analysis may not prove a thing about an author's originality or indebtedness to oral sources. An artist may be profoundly influenced by a particular mode of traditional storytelling yet not use the materials of that tradition in his own narratives. Conversely, an artist may dip deeply into the materials of oral tradition without exploiting them in a manner that could be called traditional. In short, even after the most rigorous motif analysis, we may not know much more than we did before about a writer's true debts and assets.

Our ability to document Tutuola's debt to West African oral tradition would be greatly facilitated by a comprehensive index of African tale types. A motif-index tells us nothing about narrative structure, nothing about how the motifs are strung together into tales. An index of African tale types would help us to identify the tales Tutuola has borrowed and to analyze the use he has made of them. Such investigations would do much to deepen our understanding and appreciation of Tutuola as both an oral and a literary artist. But until that ideal scholarly tool is available, we shall have to proceed like Tutuola's heroes, taking advantage of whatever resources we stumble upon as we struggle to make our way through the jungle. A motif-index is a very primitive tool, but it does allow us to cut through a few facile assumptions and glimpse some light, however dim, at the end of the trail.

The following motif-index of Amos Tutuola's *The Palm-Wine Drinkard* follows the numbering system in Thompson's *Motif-Index of Folk-Literature*. An asterisk denotes a motif that cannot be found in Thompson; the nearest Thompson number is given. Numbers in parentheses tell us how many references to a particular motif can be found in Clarke's "Motif-Index of the Folktales of Culture Area V, West Africa." Thus there are four types of entries:

A108.1.   — motif listed in Thompson but not in Clarke
A2878.*   — motif not listed in Thompson or in Clarke
B455.3.(6). — motif listed in Thompson. 6 citations in Clarke
G422.1.*(1). — motif not listed in Thompson. 1 citation in Clarke

Whenever a parenthesized number follows an index number, all of Clarke's bibliographical references are cited. Whenever a motif fits into several sections of Thompson's *Motif-Index*, cross-references are provided. Page references to *The Palm-Wine Drinkard* are given after the descriptive title of each motif.

A MOTIF-INDEX OF AMOS TUTUOLA'S
THE PALM-WINE DRINKARD

A. MYTHOLOGICAL MOTIFS

A100-A499. Gods

A108.1.   God of the dead. 12.
             A310. God of the world of the dead. A487. God of death. Z111.(5). Death personified.
A111.2.   Father of the gods. 10.
             F600. Persons with extraordinary powers.
A125.5.*   God in the appearance of an old man. 10.
A162.   Conflicts of the gods. 118-119.

A310. God of the world of the dead. 12.
   A108.1. God of the dead. A487. God of death. Z111.(5). Death personified.
A431.1.3.1.* God causes famine. 118-119.
A485. Gods of war. 46.
A487. God of death. 12.
   A108.1. God of the dead. A310. God of the world of the dead, Z111.(5). Death personified.

A2800-A2899. Miscellaneous Explanations

A2878.* Why Death wanders about in the world. 16.

B. ANIMALS

B0-B99. Mythical Animals

B15.1.* Beast with head ten times larger than body. 47.
B15.1.* Beast with head covered with sponge-like hair. 105.
B15.1.* Beast with voice sounding like a church bell. 104.
B15.2.* Beast with teeth one foot long and thick as cow's horns. 47.
B15.3.* Beast with short horns on palms. 104.
B15.3.* Beast with five curved horns on head. 47.
B15.4.2.* Beast with floodlight eyes. 54.
   B720.* Fanciful bodily members of animals.
B15.5.* Beast with hot steam rushing out of mouth and nose. 104.
B15.6.* Beast with feet like logs of wood. 47.
B15.6.* Beast with two feet on each leg. 54.
B15.6.* Beast with feet like blocks. 105.
B15.6.* Beast with fingernails two feet long. 47.
B15.7.10.* Beast with body covered with long black hair like the hair of a horse's tail. 47.
B15.7.10.* Beast with skin as sharp as sandpaper and body cold as ice. 104.
B15.7.10.* Beast with body covered with hard scales, each scale the size of a shovel. 54.
B16.3. Devastating birds. 53, 80.
   B33.(1). Man-eating birds.
B16.4.* Devastating fish carries off yearly victim. 79-80.
B31.6.* Giant red-bird with insect-covered head which weighs one ton or more. 80.
B33.(1). Man-eating birds. 53, 80.
   B16.3. Devastating birds.
   (1). Ewe: Werner 330.

B39.*   Birds with artificial heads. 52.
              B720.* Fanciful bodily members of animals.
B39.*   Bird with six teeth, each about one-half foot long. 80.
B39.*   Birds, two feet long, with one foot long beaks. 53.
B69.*   Monstrous red-fish with horns, hairy bat's body, and ability to fly.
              79-80.

B100-B199. Magic Animals

B172.   Magic bird. 76-77.
B175.(1). Magic fish. 76-77.
              (1). Kpelle: Westerman 426.

B200-B299. Animals with Human Traits

B211.2.7. Speaking sea-beast. 76.
              B211.5.(1). Speaking fish.
B211.3.   Speaking bird. 52, 76.
B211.5.(1). Speaking fish. 76.
              E211.2.7. Speaking sea-beast.
              (1). Kpelle: Westerman 426.
B214.3.*   Laughing bird. 52.
B294.*   Land-owning animal demands tribute from man who farms
              land. 48.
B299.*   Birds smoke pipes. 52.

B300-B599. Friendly Animals

B455.3.(6). Helpful eagle. 61-62.
              B520. Animal saves person's life. B544. Animal rescues captive.
              (6). Vai: Ellis 243; Radin (Ashanti: Rattray) 218; Ashanti:
              Rattray 83; Slave Coast: Trautmann 64; Kpelle: Westermann
              437; Vai: Klingenheben, ZSES XVI 97.
B498.*   Helpful bush creatures. 87-91.
              F601.1 Extraordinary companions perform hero's tasks.
B498.*   Helpful land-owning animal. 48.
B505.(2). Magic object received from animal. 48.
              D810. Magic object as a gift. D826. Magic object received from
              monster. F815.5. Extraordinary plants.
              (2). Frobenius, Atlantis XI, 200f; Nigeria: CMS III 66ff.
B520.   Animal saves person's life. 61-62.
              B455.3.(6). Helpful eagle. B544. Animal rescues captive.
B544.   Animal rescues captive. 61-62.
              B455.3.(6). Helpful eagle. B520. Animal saves person's life.

B720-B749. Fanciful Physical Qualities of Animals

B720.* Birds with artificial heads. 52.
        B39.* Other mythical birds.
B720.* Beast with floodlight eyes. 54.
        B15.4.2.* Beasts with fiery eyes.
B731.* Red-bird. 76-77.
B731.* Red-fish. 76-77.

B000-B899. Miscellaneous Animal Motifs

B872.(4). Giant bird. 80.
        G353.1.(1). Cannibal bird as ogre.
        (4). Courlander & Herzog 42; Nigeria: Herskovits, JAFL XLIV
        451; Ewe: Spieth 586; Ewe: Werner 330.
B877.* Dirty animal big as an elephant. 47.
        G369.* Monstrous ogres—miscellaneous.
B877.* "Spirit of Prey" big as a hippopotamus. 54.
        G369.* Monstrous ogres—miscellaneous.

C. TABU

C300-C399. Looking Tabu

C311.1.5. Tabu: observing supernatural helper. 86.

C600-C699. Unique Prohibitions and Compulsions.

C615. Forbidden body of water. 71.
C617. Forbidden country. 43, 51, 96.

C700-C899. Miscellaneous Tabus.

C710.* "Alives" are not allowed to enter Deads' Town. 96.

D. MAGIC

D0-D699. Transformation

D5.1. Enchanted person cannot move. 12.
D142.0.1.* Transformation: girl to kitten. 28.
D150.(7). Transformation: man to bird. 10.
        (7). Nigeria: Baumann 93; Togo: Cardinall 128; Frobenius,
        Atlantis X 221; Himmelheber 48; Sierra Leone: Migeod 312;
        Yoruba: Ogumefu 44; Slave Coast: Trautmann 52.

D151.8.*	Transformation: man to small bird. 28.
D169.*	Transformation: man to big bird like an aeroplane. 40.
D197.	Transformation: man to lizard. 26, 30.
D215.*	Transformation: woman to small red tree. 83.
D231.(5).	Transformation: man to stone. 117.

    F636.4. Remarkable stone-throw.

    (5). Tshi: Bellon 12; Tshi: Ellis 235; Meinhof 218; Radin (Ashanti: Rattray) 40; Ashanti: Rattray 197.

D255.1.	Transformation: man to canoe. 39.
D270.*	Transformation: woman to wooden doll. 108, 116.
D281.1.*	Transformation: man to air. 27.
D285.1.*	Transformation: men to fire. 81, 42.
D285.1.(1).	Transformation: man to smoke. 42.

    D573.(1). Transformation by charm.

    (1). Meinhof 217.

D397.	Transformation: lizard to person. 26-27, 30.
D431.2.(3).	Transformation: tree to person. 82-83.

    (3). Togo: Schonharl 17; Sierra Leone: Thomas 57; Slave Coast: Trautmann 95.

D432.1.	Transformation: stone to person. 117.
D435.1.*	Transformation: wooden doll to woman. 110.
D439.*	Transformation: air to person. 27.
D469.*	Transformation: matchstick to narrow bridge. 72.
D490.*	Transformation: fire to two red trees. 82.
D572.*	Transformation by use of juju. 10, 26, 39, 40, 42, 116-117.

    D630.(2). Transformation and disenchantment at will.

D573.(1).	Transformation by charm. 42.

    D285.1.(1). Transformation: man to smoke.

    (1). Yoruba: Ogumefu 4.

D630.(2).	Transformation and disenchantment at will. 10, 26, 39, 40, 42, 116-117.

    D572.* Transformation by use of juju.

    (2). Nigeria: Baumann 17; Nigeria: CMS III 46.

D642.	Transformation to escape difficult situation. 10, 26, 39, 40, 42, 116-117.

D700-D799. Disenchantment

D762.1.	Disenchantment by causing enchanted person to speak. 30.

D800-D1699. Magic Objects

D810.	Magic object a gift. 48.

    B505.(2). Magic object received from animal. D826. Magic object received from monster. F815.5. Extraordinary plants.

D812.4.1.(2).   Magic object received from the dead in lower world. 101.
                 (2). Ekoi: Talbot 236; Slave Coast: Trautmann 6f.
D816.   Magic object inherited. 9.
D826.   Magic object received from monster.
                 B505.(2). Magic object received from animal. D810. Magic
                 object as a gift. F815.5. Extraordinary plants.
D971.   Magic seed. 48.
D1024.(5).   Magic egg. 101.
                 D1470.1.8. Magic wishing-eggs.
                 (5). Gold Coast: Courlander and Prempeh 82; Liberia: Cronise
                 275, 269; Nigeria: Talbot (1932) 339; Kpelle: Westerman
                 392.
D1046.   Magic wine. 69-70.
                 D1652. Inexhaustible object.
D1273.   Magic charm. 42.
D1299.*   Magic cowrie. 22.
                 D1421. Magic object summons helper. D2020. Magic dumb-
                 ness.
D1299.*   Magic "juju-powers." 53.
                 D1380. Magic object protects.
D1336.   Magic object gives weakness. 27.
                 D2020. Magic dumbness.
D1380.   Magic object protects. 53.
                 D1299.* Magic "juju-power."
D1420.1.   Person drawn by magic spell. 57-58.
                 F151.* Road to "the Unreturnable-Heaven's Town."
D1421.   Magic object summons helper. 22.
                 D1299.* Magic cowrie. D2020. Magic dumbness.
D1470.1.8.   Magic wishing-eggs. 101, 120-121.
                 D1024.(5). Magic egg.
D1612.   Tell-tale magic objects. 28-29.
D1641.7.1.   Self-rolling head. 22.
                 R261.1.(1). Pursuit by rolling head.
D1652.   Inexhaustible object. 69-70.
                 D1046. Magic wine.
D1667.   Magic garden grows at once. 85.
                 F971.7. Sowing and reaping same day.

D1800-D2199. Manifestations of Magic Power

D1880.   Magic rejuvenation. 114.
                 E50. Resuscitation by magic. F699.* Wizard wakes man from
                 the dead.

D2020.	Magic dumbness. 22, 27.
	D1336. Magic object gives weakness. D1421. Magic object summons helper. D1299.* Magic cowrie.
D2062.2.	Blinding by magic. 35.
D2069.*	Man commands ropes of yams to bind Death and yam stakes to beat Death. 12.
D2069.*	Monstrous child prevents parents from breathing. 35.
D2069.*	Magic egg produces whips which beat ungrateful recipients of egg's bounty. 123-124.
D2089.*	Creature commands weeds to grow in a cleared cornfield. 49-50.
D2100.	Magic wealth. 121.
D2105.	Provisions magically furnished. 120-121.
D2106.	Magic multiplication of objects. 120-121.

E. THE DEAD

E0-E199. Resuscitation

E50.	Resuscitation by magic. 114.
E55.	Resuscitation by music. 84.
E105.(2).	Resuscitation by leaves. 106.
	(2). Ikom: Dayrell, RAI No. 3, 47; Ekoi: Talbot 8.

E200-E599. Ghosts and Other Revenants

E229.*	Murdered child returns from the dead. 35.
E261.1.2.	Speaking skull. 21, 22, 28, 30.
E489.*	Dead people in Deads' Town walk backwards. 97.
E489.*	Both black and white deads live in Deads' Town. 100.
	F167.14.* Otherworld inhabitants not segregated.
E489.*	Dead people do not like to see blood of the living. 97.
	F169.* Nature of the otherworld.
E489.*	Dead do not go to Deads' Town immediately. They spend two years in training in order to qualify as a full dead man. 100.
	F169.* Nature of the otherworld.

F. MARVELS

F0-F199. Otherworld Journeys

F80.(1).	Journey to lower world. 12, 77, 96.
	(1). Barker and Sinclair 89.

F81.1.2.(1). Journey to land of dead to visit deceased. 9-96.
            (1). Nigeria: Talbot (1923) 84.
F105.*   400 dead babies beat live man and woman and chase them out of Deads' town. 102.
F109.*   Live man and woman cannot enter Deads' Town in daylight. 95.
F151.*   Irresistible road draws man and woman to "the Unreturnable-Heaven's Town." 57-58.
            D1420.1. Person drawn by magic spell.
F167.14.*   Both white and black deads live in Deads' Town. 100.
            E489.* Abode of the dead—miscellaneous.
F169.*   Dead people do not like to see blood of the living. 97.
            E489.* Abode of the dead—miscellaneous.
F169.*   The dead do not go to Deads' Town immediately. They spend two years in training in order to qualify as a full dead man. 100.
            E489.* Abode of the dead—miscellaneous.
E171.   Extraordinary sights in otherword. 13.

F200-F699. Marvelous Creatures

F401.*   Creatures resembling white pillar: one-quarter mile long, six foot diameter, one eye at topmost. 42.
            F774. Extraordinary pillars.
F441.(4).   Wood-spirit. 9.
            (4). Frobenius, Atlantis XI 277f.; Himmelheber 34; Ekoi: Talbot 247; Ibibio: Talbot 78.
F460.   Mountain-spirits. 115-117.
F460.3.1.(3). Mountain-folk dance. 116.
            K772.(1). Victim enticed into dancing: captured.
            (3). Gold Coast: Courlander and Prempch 41; Yoruba: Ellis 257; Frobenius: Atlantis XI 226.
F501.*   Person consisting only of skull. 20-21.
            F559.4. Remarkable skull. G369.* Monstrous ogres.
F511.*   Person with a small head like a one-month-old baby's head. 44.
F517.1.1.(2) Person with no feet. 44.
            (2). Frobenius, Atlantis XI 291; Ekoi: Talbot 374.
F525.   Person with half a body. 35.
F527.1.   Red person. 73-83.
F529.*   Person with a lowered voice like a telephone. 35.
F531.0.4.   Giant woman. 73.
F559.4.   Remarkable skull. 20-21.
            F501.* Person consisting only of skull. G369.* Monstrous ogres.
F560.*   People treat animals better than themselves. 58-59.

F560.*	People build houses on side of steep hill so they sloped downwards. 58-59.
F560.*	People would climb ladder before leaning it against a tree. 58-59.
F570.*	"Faithful-Mother"—an old woman who helps those in difficulty. 67. N815.0.1. Tree-spirit as helper. N825.3. Old woman as helper.
F570.*	Old man walking backwards, his eyes on his knees, his arms on his thighs, chases man and woman and tries to beat them. 56.
F570.*	Refuse-covered king. 45.
F575.2.	Handsome man. 18-19.
	G410.*(2). Girl courted by transformed ogre.
F600.	Persons with extraordinary powers. 10.
	A111.2. Father of the gods.
F601.1.	Extraordinary companions perform hero's tasks. 87-91.
	B498.* Helpful bush creatures.
F611.3.2.(16)	Hero's precocious strength. 33.
	F628.0.1. Precocious strong hero as mighty slayer.
	(16). Barker & Sinclair 147; Ibo: Basden (1938) 428; Togo: Cardinall 97, 128, 165; Togo: Einstein 8; Agni: Fernor, RTP XXVII 375; Frobenius, Atlantis X 217; Togo: Hartter, ZOOS VI 135; Himmelheber 127; Lee 19; Ashanti: Rattray 49, 111; Togo: Schönhärl 31; Ekoi: Talbot 128; Ibo: Thomas, *Man* XVIII 24.
F614.*	Hero fights nine hideous creatures, kills 8 out of 9. 105-106.
F628.0.1.	Precocious strong hero as mighty slayer. 33.
	F611.3.2.(16). Hero's precocious strength.
F632.(1).	Mighty eater. 32, 87-91.
	F665. Skillful barber. F666. Skillful axe-man. F679.5. Skillful hunter.
	(1). Frobenius, Atlantis X 275.
F633.	Mighty drinker. 7, 32.
F636.4.	Remarkable stone-thrower. 117.
	D231.(5). Transformation: man to stone.
F665.	Skillful barber. 87-91.
	F632.(1). Mighty eater. F666. Skillful axe-man. F679.5. Skillful hunter.
F666.	Skillful axe-man. 87-91.
	F632.(1). Mighty eater. F665. Skillful barber. F679.5. Skillful hunter.
F679.5.	Skillful hunter. 87-91.
	F632.(1). Mighty eater. F665. Skillful barber. F666. Skillful axe-man.
F688.*	New-born child able to speak as if ten years old. 31.
	T550.2. Abnormally born child has unusual powers. T585.2.(2). Child speaks at birth. T615.1. Precocious speech.

F699.*	Child grows three feet tall within one hour. 31-32.
	T585.(3). Precocious infant. T615.(2). Supernatural growth.
F699.*	Wizard wakes man from the dead. 114.
	D1880. Magic rejuvenation. E50. Resuscitation by magic.
F699.*	A baby one day old has power to make weeds grow on king's field. 50-51.
F699.*	Child says his name is Zurrjir, which means a son who would change himself into another thing very soon. 32.
F699.*	Child finds his way home without assistance although he has never been home before. 32.
F699.*	Child recognizes and names all his relatives although he has never seen them before. 32.
F699.*	Marvelous tapper of palm trees (225 kegs per day). 7.

F700-F899. Extraordinary Places and Things

F703.	Lands with extraordinary names ("Greedy Bush"). 51-52.
	F885. Extraordinary field.
F730.	Extraordinary island ("Wraith Island"). 46-47.
	X1503. Land of Cockaygne.
F765.	City inside a tree. 68-69.
F766.	Deserted city. 55.
F768.2.	City of enchanted people. 73-74.
F771.*	Refuse-covered king's palace. 45.
F771.1.9.	House of skulls. 22.
F774.	Extraordinary pillars. 42.
	F401.* Creatures resembling white pillar.
F774.*	White pillar monsters hover around fire complaining of cold. 42.
F786.	Extraordinary chair. 22.
	R41.1.1. Captivity in subterranean palace.
F787.	Extraordinary bed. 13-14.
	F846. Extraordinary bed.
F789.*	Structure looking like a termite's house turns out to be a market. 44.
F789.*	Human bones being used by Death as firewood. 13.
F789.*	Skulls being used as basins, plates and tumblers. 13.
	F866.4. Cup made of skulls. Q491.5. Skull used as drinking cup.
F811.*	Tree which speaks and has hands which "photograph" and capture people. 65-67.
	R49.1.(1). Captivity in tree.
F811.2.*	Tree with singing leaves. 82.
F815.5.	Extraordinary seed. 48.
	B505.(2). Magic object received from animal. D810. Magic object as a gift. D826. Magic object received from monster.

F846.	Extraordinary bed. 13-14.
	F787. Extraordinary bed.
F855.	Extraordinary image. 68.
F855.*	Cream-colored female image. 44.
F855.*	Image with eyes on breasts. 55-56.
F866.4.	Cup made of skulls. 13.
	F789.* Skulls being used as basins, plates and tumblers. Q491.5. Skull used as drinking cup.
F885.	Extraordinary field. 51-52.
	F703. Land with extraordinary name.
F899.*	Bag contains a dead prince. 92-93.

F900-F1099. Extraordinary Occurrences

F911.2.(3).	Animals swallow animals. 80.
	(3). Togo: Cardinall 174; Togo: Hartter, ZOOS VI 133; Ekoi: Talbot 371.
F911.3.	Animal swallows man (not fatally). 109-110.
	R11. Abduction by monster. 110.
F912.*	Victim kills swallower from within by discharging gun in his stomach. 110.
F971.7.	Sowing and reaping same day. 85.
	D1667. Magic garden grows at once.
F979.4.(2).	Tree seizes person and lifts him up. 66-67.
	(2). Ekoi: Talbot 253; Gola: Westermann 491.
F989.*	Fishnet catches red-bird. 75.
F989.12.	Sea animal found inland. 75.
F1071.*	Skull can jump a mile a second. 22.
F1088.	Extraordinary escape. 28.
	R111.2. Princess rescued from place of captivity. R111.1.1.(1). Rescue of princess from ogre. R122. Miraculous rescue.
F1088.*	Escape by burning way to another field. 43.

G. OGRES

G10-G399. Kinds of Ogres

G11.15.	Cannibal demon. 107-108.
G15.*	Human being devoured annually. 77.
G121.1.1.	One-eyed giant (ogre). 42.
G150.*	Giant captures man and woman and puts them in bag full of strange creatures. 102.
	G441. Ogre carries victim in bag. R11.3.(1). Abduction by giant.

G150.*   Giant with enormous head. 104.
            G361. Ogre monstrous as to head.
G346.3.   Amphibious monster. 80.
            G510.4. Hero overcomes devastating monster.
G353.1.(1). Cannibal bird as ogre. 80.
            B872.(4). Giant bird.
            (1). Ewe: Werner 330.
G361.   Ogre monstrous as to head. 104.
            G150.* Giant with enormous head.
G365.   Ogre monstrous as to feet. 104.
G369.*   Ogre with two large eyes on his forehead as big as bowls. 104.
G369.*   Ogre can see a pin at a distance of three miles. 104.
G369.*   Dirty animal big as an elephant. 47.
            B877.* Giant mythical animals.
G369.*   Ogre returns parts of his body to people he rented them from and
            pays rentage. Becomes a "full-bodied gentleman reduced to
            skull." 20-21.
            F501.* Person consisting only of skull. F559.4. Remarkable
            skull.
G369.*   "Spirit of Prey" big as a hippopotamus but walking upright. 54.
            B877.* Giant mythical animal.

G400-G499. Falling into Ogre's Power

G410.*(2). Girl courted by transformed ogre. 18-19.
            F575.2. Handsome man.
            (2). Liberia: Cronise 180; Sierra Leone: Werner 251.
G422.1.*(1). Ogre has strings of drum bind victim. 12.
            (1).G422.1. Ogre imprisons victim in drum. Yoruba: Ellis 261.
G441.   Ogre carries victim in bag. 102.
            G150.* Giant captures man and woman and puts them in bag full
            of strange creatures. R11.3.(1). Abduction by giant.

G500-G599. Ogre Defeated   G600-G699. Other Ogre Motifs

G510.4,   Hero overcomes devastating animal. 80, 80.
            G346.3. Amphibious monster.
G580.*   Death overcome in fight by hero's magic. 12.
G661.   Ogre's secret overheard. 11.
            H13. Recognition by overheard conversation.
G661.1.   Ogre's secret overheard from tree. 30.

H. TESTS

H0-H199. Identity Tests: Recognition

H13.   Recognition by overheard conversation. 11-12.
           G661. Ogre's secret overheard. J1650.* Miscellaneous clever acts.

H900-H1199. Tests of Prowess: Tasks

H987.   Task performed with aid of magic object. 10, 11.
           H1272.* Quest for Death; hero brings him from his house.
           H1382. Quest for unknown objects or places.
H1049.*   Task: retrieve a man's daughter who has been captured by a curious creature.
           H1385.1. Quest for stolen princess.

H1200-H1399. Tests of Prowess: Quests

H1241.1. Hero returning from successful quest sent upon another. 11.
H1270.   Quest to lower world. 9-97.
H1272.*   Quest for Death; hero brings him from his house. 11.
           H987. Task performed with aid of magic object.
H1382.   Quest for unknown objects or places.
           H987. Task performed with aid of magic object.
H1385.1. Quest for stolen princess. 17.
           H1049.* Task: retrieve a man's daughter who has been captured by a curious creature.

J. THE WISE AND THE FOOLISH

J1100-J1699. Cleverness

J1559.*   Hero asked to judge case involving champion debitor and champion debit collector. 111-112.
           K231. Debtor refuses to pay his debt.
J1650.*   Hero transforms himself into canoe and wife paddles. They ferry people across river and earn a lot of money. 39-40.

K. DECEPTIONS

K700-K799. Capture by Deception

K735.(11). Capture in pitfall. 14.
           (11). Gold Coast: Christaller, Zs. f. Vksk. IV 70; Gold Coast:

Courlander and Prempeh 6; Frobenius: Atlantis X 290ff.; Klipple 24; Lee 24; Yoruba: Ogumefu 6, 65; Rugoff 35; Seidel 289; Temne: Schlenker 47; Ewe: Spiess 123.

K772.(1). Victim enticed into dancing: captured. 116.
F460.3.1.(3). Mountain-folk dance.
(1). Yoruba: Ellis 257 No. 4.

K2100-K2199. False Accusations

K2116.4. Murderer makes outcry so that innocent person is accused of murder. 93.

M. ORDAINING THE FUTURE

M300-M399. Prophecies

M301.* Wife of hero utters prophecies. 78, 86, 95.

M400-M499. Curses

M411.10. Curse by giant. 30.
D2021.1. Dumbness as curse. Q451.3. Loss of speech as punishment.

N. CHANCE AND FATE

N300-N399. Unlucky Accidents

N399.* Feasters break all-providing egg which then loses its power. 122.

N400-N699. Lucky Accidents

N659.* By chance a buffalo is substituted for man and wife as food for a monster. 54-55.
N660.* Rain loosens earth that man and wife are buried alive in so they can wriggle free. 62-63.
R212. Escape from grave.
N660.* Hero sleeps under bed and bed is clubbed in middle of night. 14.

N800-N899. Helpers

N800.* Eagle as helper. 61-63.
N815.0.1. Helper tree-spirit. 67.
N825.3. Old woman helper. 67.

Q. REWARDS AND PUNISHMENTS

Q10-Q99. Deeds Rewarded

Q41.(2).   Politeness rewarded. 48.
            (2). Slave Coast: Bouche 236; Gold Coast: Werner 209f.
Q53.   Reward for rescue. 30-31.

Q100-Q199. Nature of Rewards

Q114.*   Gifts: fifty kegs of palm-wine. 30-31.
Q114.*   Gift: two rooms in father-in-law's house. 30-31.
Q190.*   Reward: rescued girl as wife.

Q200-Q399. Deeds Punished

Q211.(13). Murder punished. 94-95.
            Q411.6.(9). Death as punishment for murder.
            (13). Tiv: Abraham 73; Barker and Sinclair 66; Nigeria: Dennett
            99; Frobenius: Atlantis X 273; Lee 23; Radin (Ashanti: Rattray)
            203; Ashanti: Rattray 31; Agni: Tauxier 242; Ibo: Thomas (III)
            68; Slave Coast: Trautmann 74, 76, 90; Kpelle: Westermann
            380.
Q380.*   Monstrous child killed for killing cattle and insulting relatives. 34.
            Q414. Punishment: burning alive. S11.3.3. Father kills son.
            S112. Burning to death.

Q400-Q599. Kinds of Punishment

Q411.6.(9). Death as punishment for murder. 94-95.
            Q211.(13). Murder punished.
            (9). Slave Coast: Bouche 232; Ikom: Dayrell, RAI No 3, 19, 27;
            Sierra Leone: Migeod 316; Radin (Efik-Ibibio) 496; Ashanti:
            Rattray 105; Agni: Tauxier 242; Ekoi: Talbot 334; Kpelle:
            Westermann 416.
Q414.   Punishment: burning alive. 34.
            Q380.* Monstrous child killed for killing cattle and insulting
            relatives. S11.3.3. Father kills son. S112. Burning to death.
Q451.3.   Loss of speech as punishment. 30.
            D2021.1. Dumbness as curse. M411.10. Curse by giant.
Q465.*   Burial alive as punishment. 61.
            S123.0.1. Hostages buried alive.
Q491.5.   Skull used as drinking cup. 13.
            F789.* Skulls being used as basins, plates and tumblers. F866.4.
            Cup made of skulls.

Q599.*   For killing prince, man and wife are dressed in fine clothes and put on a horse and taken around town for seven days. Then they are to be killed. 93.

R. CAPTIVES AND FUGITIVES

R0-R99. Captivity

R11.(1).   Abduction by ogre. 56-60, 109-110.
              F911.3. Animal swallows man.
              (1). Frobenius: Atlantis XI 96.
R11.1.(1).   Girl abducted. 21.
              (1).R11.* Girl lured from market to ghost home by ghost man. Ekoi: Talbot 280.
R11.3.(1).   Abduction by giant. 102.
              G150.* Giant captures man and woman and puts them in bag full of strange creatures. G441. Ogre carries victim in bag.
              (1). Agni: Tauxier 239.
R13.*   Abduction by field creatures. 44.
R41.1.1.   Captivity in subterreanean palace. 22.
              F786. Extraordinary chair.
R49.1.(1).   Captivity in tree. 65-67.
              F811.* Tree which speaks and has hands which "photograph" and capture people. 65-67.
              (1). Agni: Tauxier 239.

R100-R199. Rescues

R111.1.1.(1). Rescue of princess from ogre. 28.
              (1). Kpelle: Westermann 387.
R111.2.   Princess rescued from place of captivity. 28.
R122.   Miraculous rescue. 28.
              F1088. Extraordinary escape.

R200-R299. Escapes and Pursuits

R212.   Escape from grave. 62-63.
              N660.* Rain loosens earth in which man and woman are buried.
R219.*   Hero tells his guards, gods of war, that he is "father of gods." 46.
R219.*   Hero escapes after being left for dead. 106.
R219.*   Cannibalistic birds driven away by smell of leaves treated with "juju-power." 53.

R261.1.(1).   Pursuit by rolling head. 22.
                D1641.7.1. Self-rolling head.
                (1). Yoruba: Ellis 268.

S. UNNATURAL CRUELTY

S11.3.3.   Father kills son. 34.
                Q380.* Monstrous child killed. Q414. Punishment: burning alive. S112. Burning to death.
S21.*   Son forces parents to carry him and eats in their presence without allowing them to eat. 36-37.
S112.   Burning to death. 34.
                Q380.* Monstrous child killed. Q414. Punishment: burning alive. S11.3.3. Father kills son.
S123.0.1.   Hostages buried alive. 61-62.
                Q465.* Burial alive as punishment.
S180.*   Heads of man and woman are shaved with flat stones and pieces of broken bottle. Pepper rubbed in wounds. Fire held over wounds. Heads shaved with snail's shell. 60-61.
S186.   Torturing by beating. 58.

T. SEX

T210.*   Man with three faithful wives. 113-114.
T211.2.   Wife's suicide at husband's death. 113-114.
F541.*   Child born from thumb. 31.
T550.2.   Abnormally born child has unusual powers. 31.
T585.(3).   Precocious infant. 31-32.
                (3). Ivory Coast: Joseph, RTP XXVI 239; Ashanti: 207; Ekoi: Talbot 312.
T585.2.(3).   Child speaks at birth. 31.
                (3). Frobenius: Atlantis XI 198; Lee 19; Togo: Schönhärl 37.
T615.(2).   Supernatural growth. 31-32.
                (2). Barker and Sinclair 147; Ekoi: Talbot 33.
T615.1.   Precocious speech. 31.

V. RELIGION

V0-V99. Religious Services

V10.*   Sacrifice to juju. 23.
V11.9.   Sacrifice to deity. 124.

V12.4.5.(7). Goat as sacrifice. 23.
> (7) Ikom: Dayrell, RAI No. 3, 32, 79; Speiss 125; Ibibio: Talbot 53, 102; Ekoi: Talbot 403.

V12.4.11.(6). Bird as sacrifice. 124.
> (6). Ikom: Dayrell, RAI No. 3, 7, 32, 79; Klipple 358; Ibibio: Talbot 102; Ekoi: Talbot 403.

V12.9.*(1) Food as sacrifice. 124.
> (1). Iboi Baodon (1938) 434; Ibibio: Talbot 53, 102, Ekoi: Talbot 9.

V17.4.* Sacrifice in order to get rain. 124.

Z. MISCELLANEOUS GROUPS OF MOTIFS

Z110.* Personifications of Dance, Drum and Song lead an entire town in uninterrupted revels for two days. 84.
Z110.* Personification of Laugh. 45.
Z110.* Personifications of Drum, Dance and Song lure monstrous child away. 38-39.
Z111.(5). Death personified. 12.
> A108.1. God of the dead. A310. God of the world of the dead. A487. God of death.
>
> (5). Togo: Einstein 16f; Ashanti: Rattray 193; Liberia: Bundy, JAFL XXXII 414; Togo: Cardinall 66; Dahomey: Le Herisse 266.

Z111.1.* Death captured in a net. 15.
Z230.* Hero captures and transports Death. 15.
Z350.* Hero lends fear. 67.
Z350.* Hero sells death and is invulnerable thereafter. 67.

[1] Aarne-Thompson, intended as a practical listing of the folktales of "Europe, West Asia and the Lands Settled by These Peoples," is not very useful for the study of African tales; *The Palm-Wine Drinkard* contains variants of only two Aarne-Thompson tale types: 327C—A Monster Carries the Hero Home in a Sack (102-04), and 333—The Glutton: A monster devours human beings who later emerge alive from his belly (109-10). Klipple's doctoral dissertation is not very helpful because it does not attempt to go beyond the Aarne-

Thompson classification. The most useful African tale type indexes are those by Arewa and Lambrecht, but these cover areas other than West Africa. Prof. Dan Crowley of the University of California at Davis has been working on a comprehensive African tale type index for many years, but none of this material has been published yet.

owards an Achebe Iconography

Anna Rutherford is famous the world over as a scholar, editor, publisher, teacher, conference organizer, and ACLALS administrator, but one of her uncommon wealth of talents has not been sufficiently recognized: she is also an excellent photographer. Some of her photos have appeared from time to time in *Kunapipi* and in books issued by Dangaroo Press, and she has been very generous in supplying friends with copies of pictures she has taken of Commonwealth authors in Aarhus and elsewhere. One of her snapshots of Buchi Emecheta, published in a volume on *Twentieth-Century Caribbean and Black African Writers* that Reinhard Sander and I edited for the Dictionary of Literary Biography, is the best picture of that author I have ever seen. Emecheta, standing in front of a small London shop and looking directly at the camera, is radiantly happy and laughing. She is totally at ease, and her affection for the woman behind the camera is transparent. I doubt that any other photographer could have captured Emecheta in such a relaxed and truly delighted mood. A photo like that records the joy of genuine friendship. The beauty of the relationship is in the eye of the beheld.

But photography is not the only visual art in which Anna excels. She also has a fine sense of design. In the publications she has produced, she has made adroit use of unconventional illustrations—everything from highly stylized Aboriginal paintings to engravings taken from West Indian travel narratives to "naive" Nigerian folk art. These skillfully placed graphics have added ocular excitement to pages already rich with verbal stimulation. Original images have complemented imaginative ideas. Each new book, each new issue of *Kunapipi*, has been an adventure in seeing the world afresh.

This being the case, it would be a pity if a book intended as a tribute to Anna did not contain some interesting pictures.[1] Here are a few that I feel ought to be put into wider circulation in Anna's annals, for they are unfamiliar images of one of her favorite authors and they allow us to see him afresh.

Chinua Achebe, Nigeria's most eminent novelist, attended Government College Umuahia, reputed to be one of the best high schools in West Africa, before entering University College Ibadan in 1948. Umuahia had many strong traditions, one of which was an Old Boys' Reunion held in July each year. The earliest photos we have of Achebe as a university student are three taken at his school's Old Boys' Reunion and published in successive annual issues of *The Umuahian*. In 1951 (fig. 1) he is seated at the left end of the front row attired in a white suit. In 1952 (fig. 2) and 1953 (fig. 3) he is standing in the center of the second row wearing perhaps the same white suit. (In the 1952 photo his schoolmate Christopher Okigbo, who became one of Nigeria's finest poets, is standing at the right end of the second row wearing a hat at a rakish angle.) Achebe evidently was a loyal Old Boy who never missed a reunion and, obedient to tradition and/or economy, always dressed the same.

We have two other photos from Achebe's university days. In the first (fig. 4) he is standing between Christopher Okigbo (left) and Alex Ajayi (right). In the other (fig. 5) he is pictured with members of the 1952-53 Editorial Board of the *University Herald*; Achebe, Editor-in-Chief, is seated at the left end beside Vincent Chukwuemeka Ike, who also later rose to prominence as a novelist. Both Achebe and Ike wrote regularly for the *University Herald*, publishing their first short stories and essays there.

The next photo (fig. 6), taken in 1964, shows Achebe working in Lagos as Director of the Voice of Nigeria. By this time his first three novels—*Things Fall Apart* (1958), *No Longer at Ease* (1960), and *Arrow of God* (1964)—would have been published.

These photos give us a sense of how young Achebe was when he started his writing career. In 1951, when the first Old Boys' Reunion shot was taken, he would have been 20 years old. In 1964, with three major works behind him, he would have been only 33.

The rest of the images are caricatures, all but one of which appeared in the Nigerian press in the 1980s and 1990s. Four of them were drawn for Nigeria's leading literary newspaper, *The Guardian*, by cartoonists Cliff Ogiugo (fig. 7), Tony Olise (fig. 8), Ake Didi Onu (fig. 9), and Obe Ess (fig. 10). Achebe and other prominent local literary personalities (especially Nobel Prize winner Wole Soyinka) are frequently caricatured in the Nigerian press.

The final image (fig. 11) may provide irrefutable evidence of Achebe's literary canonization in the West. It was drawn by David Levine, the cartoonist for the *New York Review of Books*, to accompany a review (published on 3 March 1988) of Achebe's novel *Anthills of the Savannah*.[2] To be drawn by Levine, even in an unflattering manner, is considered a rare honor. He has sketched many of the leading personalities of contemporary times as well as a good number of the literary, political, sports and entertainment giants of the past—everyone from Winston Churchill to Walt Disney, Charles de Gaulle to Princess Di, Leonardo da Vinci to Muhammad Ali, Sigmund Freud to Woody Allen. Among the literary "immortals" who have been cut down to size by his witty strokes are Brecht, Conrad, T.S. Eliot, F. Scott Fitzgerald, Gogol, Hemingway, Henry James, Joyce, Kipling, Milton, Pope, Pound, Sartre, Shakespeare, Stendahl, Voltaire, Wilde, Wordsworth and Zola. Needless to say, this places Achebe in very distinguished company indeed. But in one respect he is ahead of all the rest. Achebe is the only author in the entire group shown seated before a computer!

*F*igure 1: *Old Boys's Reunion, 1951 (Achebe seated at far left; Christopher Okigbo in middle row, third from far right). Photo: Government College,* Umuahia Magazine.

*F*igure 2: *Old Boys' Reunion, 1952 (Achebe standing, seventh from right).* Photo: *Government College,* Umuahia Magazine.

*F*igure 3: *Achebe (centre, rear) at Old Boys' Reunion, Government College Umuahia, 1953. Photo: Government College,* Umuahia Magazine.

*F*igure 4: *Christopher Okigbo, Chinua Achebe and Alex Ajayi as students at University College, Ibadan. Photo: Chinua Achebe.*

*F*igure 5: *Editorial Board,* University Herald, *Ibadan, 1952–53*
(Achebe at far left). Photo: Chinua Achebe.

*F*igure 6: *Director of the Voice of Nigeria, Lagos, 1964.*
Photo: Chinua Achebe.

F *igure 7: Chinua Achebe.*
Caricature by Cliff Ogiugo of the Guardian *(Lagos).*

F *igure 8: Chinua Achebe.*
Caricature by Tony Olise of the Guardian *(Lagos).*

*F*igure 9: *Chinua Achebe.*
Caricature by Ake Didi Onu of the Guardian *(Lagos).*

*F*igure 10: *Chinua Achebe.*
Caricature by Obo Ess of the Guardian *(Lagos).*

*F*igure 11: *Chinua Achebe. Caricature by David Levine,*
New York Review of Books, *3 March 1988.*

[1] This essay originally appeared in a festschrift for Rutherford entitled *A Talent(ed) Digger*, edited by Maes-Jelinek, Collier and Davis.

[2] A copy of the Levine caricature, matted and framed (17" x 21"), may be purchased for $85, plus handling and shipping, from Satire Press, 185 Prospect Park SW, Suite 602, Brooklyn, NY 11218.

Contexts

Are There Any National Literatures in Black Africa Yet?

The simple answer is no. Judged by any of the standard criteria for measuring the "nationality" of a literature—language, subject matter, style, ideas, audience, quantity and quality of output, integrity of worldview—modern African literatures fall far short of qualifying for full-scale literary independence. Most of them are much too young and too small to have developed their own distinguishing characteristics, and those few that have matured to the point of no longer being inconspicuous in the commonwealth of world letters are still growing so fast that their configurations could change considerably in the next half-century. It is difficult to speak of "traditions" or distinctive national features in literatures so young and mutable. A longer span of time is needed to define a nation's literary individuality.

In sub-Saharan Africa the situation is complicated by ambiguities underlying the concept of nationhood itself. Hardly any African nations are more than forty years old, and many have undergone profound social and political transformations since acquiring independence. In some areas there have been frequent changes of government, often accomplished by military coups and counter-coups or occasionally—as in Nigeria, Ethiopia, Rwanda, Burundi, Uganda and Zaïre—by outright civil war. To what country does a citizen caught in the midst of one of these conflicts pledge his allegiance? Is patriotism possible in such turmoil? Does nationhood have any meaning in internally divided nations?

Historians and political scientists will point out that there are perfectly good explanations for the instability that has beset so many African states. One is that Africans played no role in determining the boundaries of the polities that were established in Africa at the end of the nineteenth century to keep European colonial powers from squabbling over unclaimed or disputed territory. The European statesmen who attended the Berlin Conference of 1884-85 simply drew lines on a map and carved up the continent to serve their own national interests rather than the interests of the peoples who happened to be living there. This diplomatic land-grab had rather remarkable consequences in certain areas. For instance, the Ewe, a tribe living along what was known as the Gold Coast of West Africa, found itself divided among three different European colonial powers: England, Germany and France. In Nigeria—indeed, in most West African colonies that stretched northward as far as the sands of the Sahara—numerous tribes with totally dissimilar cultures, traditions and religious beliefs were administered as one corporate entity. African "colonies" were really administrative fictions with nothing holding them together but the bureaucratic imagination and territorial appetite of the colonizers. When these artificially created ethnic conglomerates later became independent African nation-states recognized and seated at the U.N., there was seldom any serious discussion of the possibility of dismantling and reorganizing them more rationally. The winds of change which had swept across the African continent after the second World War could not alter the old arbitrary boundary lines drawn in Berlin. Accidents of nineteenth-century European cartography thus determined twentieth-century African political realities, which too often led to conflict and disorder. The spirit of African nationalism that finally brought an end to colonialism degenerated in some countries into factionalism or competing ethnic nationalisms. History, it seemed, had played a cruel joke on sub-Saharan Africa.

One of the greatest obstacles to unity in most parts of Africa has been linguistic diversity. It is estimated that there are over a thousand languages spoken in Africa, perhaps as many as four hundred of them in Nigeria alone. To this incredible babble of tongues the European colonizer added his own, enshrining it as the official language in each of his colonies and using it to conduct the affairs of government, justice and foreign trade.

When schools were established for Africans, instruction at all levels in the French colonies and at all but the most elementary levels in the English colonies was carried out in the colonial tongue. Since the majority of these schools were set up by missionaries, religious indoctrination was a major objective of the educational program. To learn English or French meant to learn Christianity as well. Indeed, baptism was often a prerequisite for admission to school. Many Africans could not obtain a Western education without providing evidence that they had already pledged their souls to the new culture.

The literary consequences of political and religious colonialism in Africa are quite obvious today. The unwillingness or inability of church and state institutions to cope with the linguistic diversity of Africa is reflected in the fact that creative literature has been produced in scarcely more than fifty African languages. Furthermore, according to a survey conducted by Jahn, 58% of all creative literary works in African vernaculars have been published in only six languages: Southern Sotho, Xhosa, Zulu, Northern Sotho (including Pedi), Swahili and Yoruba (228). It is significant that four of these languages are situated in southern Africa where, largely for political reasons, there has been a long tradition of education (extending even to tertiary education) in African languages. In contrast, as Jahn points out, "there is no literature in an African language in Portuguese Africa and hardly any in French-speaking areas" (228). Needless to say, African languages were not used as the medium of instruction in colonial schools in these areas.

If one examines the development of the African language literatures that do exist, one is struck by certain recurring tendencies. Many of the books produced, particularly the early works, are of a preponderantly moralistic nature. Sometimes they are retellings of folk stories or Bible stories, sometimes imitations of European religious literature, sometimes both. The first works of fiction in Southern Sotho, Yoruba and Ibo were episodic narratives modeled on John Bunyan's *The Pilgrim's Progress* but molded from traditional motifs and materials (for details see Kunene, Bamgbose, and Emenyonu). Some of the earliest creative writing in Kikongo blended the form of the church hymn with that of the oral praise poem (Mbelolo ya Mpiku). In African language literatures influenced by Arab culture—Hausa and Swahili, for instance—the same kind of heavy moral emphasis was often present, though the literary models were far more likely to be Arab than Western, with the Koran and *The Thousand and One Nights* displacing the Bible and *The Pilgrim's Progress* as the most influential texts (Skinner, Harries). The author's motive for writing was primarily didactic; he sought to instruct more than to entertain, though he was not necessarily averse to making his instruction highly entertaining.

Such literature, particularly in the Christian areas, was addressed to a young audience. This was perhaps inevitable, for the first publishers of books in the vernacular were usually mission presses which had been set up to promote literacy in African languages so that Africans could read the Word of God for themselves. These presses encouraged mission-educated Africans to write stories and essays that could be printed and used as instructional material in the mission schools. Early creative writing in most African languages thus tended to be the kind of literature that helped to reinforce the religious message that the missionaries were trying to impart to the young. It had to be addressed to a school audience because there was no other. Not until the school had trained several generations of students did a sizable adult reading audience outside the mission station exist. And even then, publishing in African languages continued to be monopolized or controlled by the mission presses so certain kinds of adult literature were still unthinkable—or at least unpublishable. The African who chose to write in his mother tongue thus had very rigid constraints on his creativity which inhibited his growth and development as a writer. Even today, with state and private publishers competing with the mission presses in some countries, the major market for books in African languages remains the schools in which these languages are utilized and taught.

The African whose education enabled him to write in a European language faced a different set of problems. He was freer to create an adult literature, but until quite recently, he found it necessary to write primarily for a foreign audience. During the colonial era, few indigenous publishing houses were established in Africa, so the first African authors to write books in English, French and Portuguese had to send their manuscripts to London, Paris or Lisbon to get them published. Since these books were sold mainly in Europe, the aspiring author had to ensure that his message would be intelligible to non-African readers abroad. This often meant overloading his work with anthropological information and providing lengthy translations of words and concepts unknown to Europeans. No shortcuts for the benefit of African readers were permitted. After all, a novel, play or collection of poetry issued in an expensive hardcover edition in a faraway land would remain virtually out of reach of most Africans anyway.

Although Africans writing in European languages have many more opportunities today to publish their works in Africa, the problem of reaching an indigenous audience persists. Most African countries still have very high rates of illiteracy, and the number of educated Africans who read literary works in a European language for pleasure is still quite small (Achebe 1972). The African author who tries to address himself to his own people in English, French or Portuguese is therefore speaking only to a tiny elite, some of whom have no desire to listen. The only way he can catch the ear of a substantial number of his educated countrymen is by writing the kind of book that will get adopted as a prescribed text for high school and university literature examinations. Ironically, only then will his writings begin to make an impact on his own people on a truly national scale.

Chinua Achebe, defending the African writer's option to make literary use of a European tongue, has argued that

A national literature is one that takes the whole nation for its province and has a realised or potential audience throughout its territory. In other words a literature that is written in the *national* language. An ethnic literature is one which is available only to one ethnic group within the nation. If you take Nigeria as an example, the national literature, as I see it, is the literature written in English; and the ethnic literatures are in Hausa, Ibo, Yoruba, Efik, Edo, Ijaw, etc., etc.

Achebe then went on to offer a very pragmatic reason for writing in English:

The real question is not whether Africans *could* write in English but whether they *ought to*. Is it right that a man should abandon his mother-tongue for someone else's? It looks like a dreadful betrayal and produces a guilty feeling. But for me there is no other choice. I have been given this language and I intend to use it. (1965: 27, 30)

While it is certainly true that English gives a Nigerian writer a larger potential audience in his own country than any "ethnic" language could, one has to remember that this audience consists only of a relatively small percentage of those Nigerians who have had sufficient formal education to acquire a competence in the former colonial tongue. In other words, one's readership is limited to a certain stratum in society—the highly educated, Westernized upper-class. One is not really creating a literature for the masses but rather a literature for the select few. This is perhaps a more "dreadful betrayal" of one's nation than writing in an ethnic tongue for a geographically limited but more socially diversified audience would be. One is simply choosing to address oneself to a different minority.

Of course, it would be impossible for an African writer to write for everyone in his country. There is no way he could guarantee himself a national audience even if his works were to be translated and published (or broadcast) in every language in the nation. A "national literature" presupposes a national experience which is unique and distinguishable from national experiences elsewhere. Most African nations are so heterogeneous in population and consequently so incredibly complicated in social structure, political organization and historical development that the experiences of one group in the society will not always be representative of those of all other groups in the society. If a writer elects to treat a theme such as birth, marriage or death—to mention only the most basic possibilities—he will have to set it in a special social context which will immediately make it uncharacteristic of groups which exist in very different social circumstances. The Yoruba do not marry as the Hausa do. The educated Ibo do not necessarily worship the same gods as the uneducated Ibo. To write a literary work specific to one of the many subcultures in Nigeria is therefore not quite the same thing as writing a Nigerian national epic. It will express only one facet of a multi-faceted society.

If one attempts to write on a larger theme and describe an experience common to many of the cultures in the country— e.g., the encounter between colonizer and colonized, the tribulations of the Westernized African who finds himself a "man of two worlds," the mixed results of political independence—it will be equally difficult to compose an exclusively national epic because these experiences will have been shared by similar groups in many other African nations, especially those nearby. The Ghanaian colonial experience was not fundamentally different from the Nigerian. French schooling in Senegal followed the same pattern and had the same cultural impact as French schooling in the Ivory Coast and the Cameroons. If writers in such countries deal with similar subjects in similar ways, they will be creating a regional literature—i.e., a West African literature—rather than a national literature. Such literatures may split along linguistic rather than geographical or political lines— e.g., West African literature in English might be distinguished more easily from West African literature in French than from East African literature in English—but it will remain exceedingly difficult to sort them all out individually and define the unique nationality of each and every one. Wellek and Warren commented on this kind of difficulty in their *Theory of Literature*:

> Problems of "nationality" become especially complicated if we have to decide that literatures in the same language are distinct national literatures, as American and modern Irish assuredly are. Such a question as why Goldsmith, Sterne, and Sheridan do not belong to Irish literature, while Yeats and Joyce do, needs an answer. Are there independent Belgian, Swiss, and Austrian literatures? It is not very easy to determine the point at which literature written in America ceased to be "colonial English" and became an independent national literature. Is it the mere fact of political independence? Is it the national consciousness of the authors themselves? Is it the use of national subject matter and "local color"? Or is it the rise of a definite national literary style?
>
> Only when we have reached decisions on these problems shall we be able to write histories of national literature which are not simply geographical or linguistic categories, shall we be able to analyze the exact way in which each national literature enters into European tradition. Universal and national literatures implicate each other. A pervading European convention is modified in each country: there are also centers of tradition in the individual countries, and eccentric and individually great figures who set off one national tradition from the other. To be able to describe the exact share of the one and the other would amount to knowing much that is worth knowing in the whole of literary history. (41-42)

I submit that in Africa today it is not yet possible to make such discriminations in a valid and meaningful way.

I would go further and say that with one or two possible exceptions African literatures in African languages do not ever stand a chance of becoming national literatures. They will remain ethnic literatures feeding and enriching the elite literature of the nation which inevitably will be written in a European language. Only if the political boundaries of Africa are changed to conform with the territory occupied by major language groups will truly national literatures in African languages become something more than a chimera.

The two possible exceptions are Southern Sotho literature in Lesotho and Swahili literature in Tanzania. Lesotho, one of the smallest nations in Africa, is one of the few in which a single African language predominates. It also has a relatively long literary history extending over a century, during which at least one major writer evolved—Thomas Mofolo (Gérard 101-08). Unfortunately, Lesotho is a little too small for its own literature. According to Jahn and Dressler's *Bibliography of Creative African Writing*, more than 40% of the works produced in Southern Sotho have been written by authors from the Republic of South Africa, where Southern Sotho is one of the major ethnic languages. Unless Lesotho, which became an independent nation in 1966, can produce a literature in Southern Sotho that is distinctively different from that produced in the Republic of South Africa, any claim that it is producing its own unique national literature will have questionable validity. One may of necessity be forced either to ignore political boundaries and speak of Southern Sotho literature (as most scholars do) or else to recognize the boundaries and speak of the literature (or literatures) of Lesotho and the Basotho diaspora.

The other major African language literatures in southern Africa are in precisely the opposite position. All are housed completely or largely in a single state—the Republic of South Africa. Not one could legitimately claim national literary status unless the territory it occupies were somehow to become detached from the Republic and gain recognition as an independent African state—an infinitely remote possibility at best. Even Tswana literature remains politically amorphous, most of it being produced by writers in the Republic rather than in Botswana, its putative home. The literary situation in Swaziland, another tiny self-governing state in the south, is impossible to assess because it has not yet produced any significant quantity of literature.

In Tanzania Swahili literature enjoys a favored position because Swahili has been officially adopted as the national language. It is the mother-tongue of Tanzanians living along the coast and on the island of Zanzibar, and it has become a lingua franca in the interior among Bantu peoples who speak it as a second or third language. Indeed, it has spread as a vehicular language throughout Kenya (where it is also a national language and the mother-tongue of certain coastal peoples), Uganda, eastern Zaïre and northern Malawi, but only in Tanzania and Kenya has a substantial body of Swahili literature grown up over the past two hundred years. Whether these writings should be discussed as separate national literatures, a single ethnic literature or something else is a question that Swahili scholars have debated. Lyndon Harries has argued that "Swahili literature does not represent the cultural achievements of the Kenyans or the Tanzanians as a whole; nor does it share the same origins as gave rise to the Kenyan or Tanzanian sense of nationhood...In both Kenya and Tanzania the Swahili subculture is only one of many" (39). Moreover, since the island of Zanzibar was producing Swahili manuscripts long before it united with Tanganyika in 1964 to form the nation known now as Tanzania, one could ask if this island's early literature should be classified today as Tanzanian or Zanzibari? This may be splitting hairs, but it is a question that must be addressed by anyone who seriously maintains that Tanzania already possesses a *national* literature of considerable antiquity written in Swahili. One would also have to weigh the evidence that "up-country" Tanzanians do not identify with Swahili literature, which they find very difficult to read. According to Harries, "they don't feel that the poetry is addressed to them or that it belongs to them; it belongs only to those who are the real Swahilis (*Waswahili hasa*)" (62). If Swahili literature belongs only to the "real Swahilis," can it be considered a national literature? The logical answer appears to be: "No—at least, not yet." However, given circumstances which continue to favor its growth and development as a medium of popular cultural expression, it is conceivable that Swahili literature might ultimately achieve genuine national stature not only in Tanzania but perhaps in Kenya as well.

The literatures in European languages in Africa are also likely to grow in importance as literacy spreads and educational opportunities increase and multiply. More readers will mean more writers, and more writers will eventually mean more fully developed literatures. Regional configurations will gradually break down into pronounced national patterns capable of being distinguished from one another. How long this process of individuation will take depends on a variety of extraliterary factors such as economic growth, political and social change, etc.—factors that often defy reliable prediction. All that seems clear at this point is that some African national literatures will emerge more rapidly than others.

Two are already approaching the threshold of maturity: Nigerian literature in English and South African literature in English. Nigeria, with a population today of one hundred million, has been Africa's most prolific producer of English language literature for the past forty years, partly because it has more novelists, playwrights, poets and short story writers than any other African nation. Several of these writers are well-known outside Africa, and one of them, Wole Soyinka, has already won the Nobel Prize for Literature. In quality as well as quantity of literary output, Nigeria is leading the continent.

Nigerian literature in English has also been extraordinarily diversified, yet definite trends and tendencies are now slowly becoming discernible. It has dealt with problems of the past as well as problems of the present and has reflected in its evolution the contemporary history of Africa from precolonial and independence eras to the current post-colonial period. If has, in other words, articulated Nigerian responses to events and experiences which, while typical of much of the African subcontinent, took specific Nigerian forms. It has already treated in some depth the most traumatic of these historic happenings— the Nigerian civil war—which was quite unlike any other armed conflict ever to have occurred in Africa. The amount of writing generated in Nigeria by the war has by now turned Nigerian literature in a direction decidedly different from that of other West African literatures. Nigerian writing seems destined to continue to reflect the uniqueness of Nigerian national experience.

Moreover, with the passage of time it is becoming increasingly possible to define characteristically Nigerian literary themes, forms and styles. The reappraisal of the African past was a common theme during the colonial and early independence eras, giving way in the mid-1960s to exposés of post-colonial corruption and political mismanagement and then in the early 1970s to post-mortems on the civil war. The poets who emerged at Nsukka prior to the war are, as a group, distinguishable from the first generation of poets who made their appearance in the late 1950s at Ibadan. The Ibo novelists who initially followed in the footsteps of Achebe can be described as a school of writers making use of ideas and techniques introduced by one master teacher. Ibo writers and Yoruba writers tend to express themselves quite differently in English, even when approaching identical subjects in identical literary forms. Of late, writers in southern parts of the country have devoted a lot of attention to the power politics of military rule. Out of such gross generalizations tempered by many fine distinctions it may be possible someday to write a history of Nigerian literature in English, acknowledging it as the first true national literature in sub-Saharan Africa.

Black South African literature in English, on the other hand, may achieve distinctiveness because it encompasses what could be considered as the first African national literature in exile. Many of the major "non-white" South African writers—Peter Abrahams, Alex La Guma, Dennis Brutus, Mazisi Kunene, Es'kia Mphahlele, Lewis Nkosi, Keorapetse Kgositsile—have spent their most productive years living in Europe or the United States. Several—Bloke Modisane, Arthur Nortje, Nat Nakasa, Alfred Hutchinson—have died abroad. These writers have all been passionately committed to social and political change in South

Africa and have sought through their writings to make the outside world aware of the injustice and inhumanity of the apartheid system. A tradition of autobiographical narrative developed among them, partly to satisfy public curiosity in Europe and America about the lives of oppressed blacks in an African society ruled until recently by whites and partly to relieve the writers' pent-up feelings of bitterness and frustration so they can begin to function effectively in exile. While they were living in South Africa, these writers wrote mainly short stories and poems, but upon leaving their homeland, many of them began to experiment with longer and more complex literary forms: the novel, the play, the epic poem, as well as the autobiography. Meanwhile, the black writers remaining in South Africa have continued to express themselves primarily in short, intense forms: the short story, the improvised oral poem, the essay.

As one might expect, much black South African writing in English has been protest literature, but before the 1990s strict censorship laws made it virtually impossible for writers there to voice strong protest openly. Since the exiled writers were banned and could not legally be published, quoted or read in South Africa, their protest never reached a home audience. The result of this peculiar set of circumstances has been that an anti-apartheid national literature grew up outside the country but had only a foreign readership, while the literature produced by black writers inside South Africa was so emasculated by government censorship that it could not be said to express accurately the will and spirit of those by whom and for whom it was created. Today, with the historic dismantling of apartheid and concomitant conversion of South Africa into a truly democratic multiracial nation, an entirely new chapter in the nation's literary history is about to be written, and no doubt it will be entirely different from what has gone before. So the uniqueness of the South African situation, past and present, more than likely will generate a totally unique literature that stands a chance of becoming something that could be called "national," albeit produced at one stage of its development largely on foreign soil.

Returning now to the original question—are there any national literatures in sub-Saharan black Africa yet?—the simple answer is still no; but a fuller answer that takes into account the linguistic, political and literary complexity of the subcontinent would have to be: "No, but perhaps there will be a few fairly soon."

Politics, Culture, and Literary Form

The new literatures in English and French that have emerged in black Africa in the twentieth century have been profoundly influenced by politics. Indeed, one could argue that they have been generated and shaped by the same forces that have transformed much of the African continent during the past hundred years. Writers have served not only as chroniclers of contemporary political history but also as advocates of radical social change. Their works thus both reflect and project the course of Africa's cultural revolution.

Paradoxically, an African literature written in a European language is likely to be a more accurate barometer of fluctuations in national circumstances and mood than a literature written in an African language. One of the ironies of multilingualism in Africa is that the extraordinary number and variety of languages in most sub-Saharan nations make communication across ethnic and international boundaries difficult in anything but a colonial tongue. The writer who chooses to express himself in an African language will be addressing his message to a relatively small audience, merely a fraction of the total literate population in his country. Moreover, he may have to submit his work to prior censorship by church or state because missionary and government publishers may offer the only opportunities for publication in that language. Since such publishers tend to be interested primarily in providing reading matter for use in schools, an aspiring author may find himself compelled to write for young people instead of adults. In other words, he may be tongue-tied by the institutional constraints that inhibit open literary expression in his mother tongue.

An African author who chooses to write in a colonial language—particularly English or French—will be able to reach a much larger audience both at home and abroad and will not be prevented from articulating mature ideas that the church, state or school finds offensive. As a consequence, what he writes will be far more representative of the intellectual climate of his time and place than anything written in a local language for a smaller, younger and less heterogeneous audience. He will be addressing a national audience because he will be communicating in a national language rather than an ethnic idiom (Achebe 1965: 27-30), and the international scope of his adopted tongue will carry his voice still farther. Only through European linguistic means will he be able to work effectively toward pan-African ends.

The Negritude writers were the first to prove this point. When asked why he and other francophone African poets wrote in French, Léopold Sédar Senghor replied:

> Because we are cultural half-castes, because, although we feel as Africans, we express ourselves as Frenchmen, because French is a language with a universal vocation, because our message is addressed to the Frenchmen of France as well as to other men, because French is a language of 'graciousness and civility"...I know what its resources are because I have tasted and digested and taught it, and it is a language of the gods. Listen to Corneille, Lautréamont, Rimbaud, Péguy and Claudel. Listen to the great Hugo. The French language is a mighty organ capable of all tones and of all effects, from the softest mildness to the fulgurations of the storm. It is one by one, or all together, flute and oboe, trumpet and cannon. Again, French has given us the gift of its abstract words, so rare in our mother tongues, by which tears turn into precious stones. With us, words are naturally surrounded by an aura of sap and blood. French words are radiant with a thousand fires, like diamonds. Flares lighting up our night (94-95)

It was necessary to use such a combustible vehicle to bring home the explosive cultural message of Negritude "to the Frenchmen of France as well as to other men." Only a "language of the gods" could fully express the nuances of the new mythology that the "cultural half-castes" of French West Africa and the Antilles were beginning to propagate. Senghor and his apostles knew that one couldn't win converts to a syncretic pan-Negro faith by preaching only in Serer. The flares of French were needed to bring light to the entire black diaspora.

It is significant that the literary form chosen most often to carry this message was the surrealist poem. This form, with its powerful analogical strategies of rhythm, image and symbol, not only epitomized what Senghor regarded as the essence of African verbal art (Bâ), it also simultaneously linked African creativity with a respected, albeit once avant-garde, mode of European poetic expression. Negritude poetry was thus something both new and old, both freshly inventive yet recognizably imitative, a cross-cultural poetry in a quasi-familiar hybrid form that blended and synthesized two disparate artistic traditions into a harmoniously integrated whole. Like the poets themselves, Negritude poems were cultural assimilados readily accepted in French intellectual circles. They may have appeared quaint and picturesque to some European readers (Senghor 90-91), but their very accessible exoticism made them quite exciting to others. The ideology of Negritude probably would not have made such a strong impact on the French-speaking world had it not been packaged in such an impeccably "civilized" form. Surrealism was a very elegant mode of protest.

The Negritude poets were thus proving their right to be taken seriously by introducing new ideas in a manner Europe understood and appreciated. Their argument had philosophical depth, interesting cultural implications, and rock-hard Cartesian lucidity. Like leaders of earlier French intellectual movements, the founding fathers of Negritude had issued a manifesto and were proceeding to generate literary evidence to support their position. Since surrealist poetry alone could not convey their ideas with sufficient precision, they also wrote essays attempting to define and elaborate key concepts. These efforts paid off handsomely. In no time at all Negritude gained recognition as both an ideology and a mystique in the best French dialectical tradition.

Even latter-day critics of Negritude—and there are many, particularly in anglophone Africa—acknowledge its historical importance. Most would agree with Stanislas Adotevi's assertion that

> although certain aspects may seem old-fashioned and with frankly reactionary objectives, we should consider [the era of Negritude] as a primitive period necessary to the African renaissance...At a time when the whole world was given over to racialism...at a time when the whole of humanity raised voice in competitive cacophony, there was a single pistol-shot in the middle of this concert— negritude. It shook a few consciences and brought a few negroes together, and this was a good thing." (74-75)

However, it is doubtful that this shot would have made such an impact if the pistol had been manufactured entirely in Africa. It took a European instrument in skilled African hands to shock the world into greater awareness of the humanity of colonized black peoples.

After Negritude had done its work, the surrealist poem and philosophical essay gave way in French West Africa to another literary form: the satirical novel. Anti-colonial humor in fiction by Mongo Beti, Ferdinand Oyono, Bernard Dadié, and even Camara Laye (in some of the lugubriously hallucinated episodes in *Le Regard du roi*) set the dominant tone of the 1950s. The change in form and mood suited the temper of the times. Now that colonialism was moribund, one could afford to laugh at colonizer and colonized alike, pointing out absurd aspects of their interaction. Since it was no longer necessary to demonstrate that Africans were human beings, one could relax a bit and depict them as no better and no worse than Europeans, who certainly weren't saints. One didn't have to romanticize the past or pretend that villages in Africa were more wholesome morally than cities in Europe. The fact that independence was just around the corner made self-confident self-criticism and joking possible. Instead of striving to impress the colonial master, one now had license to tickle him, even if the last laugh was at his own expense. Satirical fiction may have helped to ease social and political tensions in French West Africa prior to independence by comically deflating some the issues that had been blown out of proportion during the Negritude era. The ironic needle now spoke louder than the pistol-shot.

In English-speaking West Africa the novel also emerged as the dominant literary form at the end of the colonial period, but it was a very different kind of novel. Writers there were more serious about their work and seldom cracked a smile. Like the earlier Negritude advocates, they sought to create a dignified image of the African past, but they were careful not to glorify the precolonial era as a Golden Age. According to Chinua Achebe, the most influential novelist of this period, the best way to "plead the cause of the past" was to project an "accurate but maybe unexciting image," not a romanticized one "which though beautiful is a distortion." It was simply a matter of effective tactics. Achebe felt that

> the credibility of the world [the writer] is attempting to recreate will be called to question and he will defeat his own purpose if he is suspected of glossing over inconvenient facts. We cannot pretend that our past was one long, technicolour idyll. We have to admit that like any other people's past ours had its good as well as its bad sides. ("Role" 158)

Yet the kind of objectivity that Achebe and his followers tried to achieve in depicting traditional African village life was not devoid of political commitment. The writer was expected to argue a case against colonialism by showing the damage it had done in Africa. The novelist in particular was regarded as a teacher whose primary task was to reeducate his society to an acceptance of itself. He could accomplish this by strongly affirming the value of African culture. Achebe believed that the "fundamental theme" of the African writer should be

> that African peoples did not hear of culture for the first time from Europeans; that their societies were not mindless but frequently had a philosophy of great depth and value and beauty, that they had poetry and, above all, they had dignity. It is this dignity that many African peoples all but lost during the colonial period, and it is this that they must now regain. The worst thing that can happen to any people is the loss of their dignity and self-respect. The writer's duty is to help them regain it by showing them in human terms what happened to them, what they lost. ("Role" 157)

He could do this best by writing realistic fiction.

Most of the early anglophone West African novelists wrote sad stories of culture conflict. They would either show how a well-knit African community became divided after exposure to Western institutions such as the church and school or else reveal how individuals suffered psychological distress because they had become "men of two worlds" who could not reconcile the African and Western elements of their personality. Either things fell apart in the villages or people fell apart in the cities. In both cases Africa was no longer at ease because a collision with Europe had knocked it off balance. The legacy of colonialism was cultural confusion, and it was virtually impossible to find stable moral values in societies or individuals mired in such a mess. Contrary to Western colonial mythology, Europe did not bring light, peace and justice to the Dark Continent; it brought chaos to what had once been a well-ordered world. This was the theme that preoccupied the first generation of anglophone West African novelists. They were attempting to rewrite African history in their fiction, and to do so effectively, they chose to express themselves in a manner that could not be misunderstood. Plain prose was a more powerful mode of protest for them than abstract poetry.

By the mid-1960s, only a few years after independence had been achieved, the popular mood in West Africa had changed to such an extent that new political institutions began to spring up to supplant the parliamentary forms of democracy hastily bequeathed to Africa as Europe departed. First it was the one-party state, then the military junta, that dominated the scene. Africans who had followed their nationalist leaders into independence became disenchanted with them afterwards and sought to bring them down. Since increasing centralization of power within the new nation-state made this difficult to accomplish through constitutional means, the army often played a key role in effecting political change. Bullets replaced ballots as instruments of governance, and in at least one country post-coup conflicts deteriorated into full-scale civil war. The pre-independence dream of a brave new world had turned into a nasty postcolonial nightmare.

During this period West African writers could not ignore what they saw around them. The novel remained their major literary outlet but they used it now as a vehicle of strong social and political satire. Instead of continuing to reconstruct the dignity of the African past, they turned their attention to the ugliness of the present and began to point the finger of blame at Africans themselves instead of Europeans. Wole Soyinka, who switched from drama to fiction during this period, exclaimed that "the African writer needs an urgent release from the fascination of the past" if he is to fulfill his function "as the record of the mores and experience of his society *and* as the voice of vision in his own time" (13). Chinua Achebe agreed, pointing out that

> Most of Africa today is politically free; there are thirty-six independent African States managing their own affairs— sometimes quite badly. A new situation has thus arisen. One of the writer's main functions has always been to expose and attack injustice. Should we keep at the old theme of racial injustice (sore

as it still is) when new injustices have sprouted all around us? I think not.

The "black writer's burden," Achebe argued, was "to express our thought and feeling, even against ourselves, without the anxiety that what we say will be taken as evidence against our race" ("Burden" 138-39). In other words, the political battle at home was now far more important than the cultural struggle abroad.

This new emphasis continued into the 1970s, with novelists alternating between slice-of-life realism and sardonic satire. In Nigeria, where more novels were produced than in any other West African nation, the center of focus became the civil war experience. It is not surprising that most of this fiction was written by Ibos, many of whom used Biafran soldiers as their heroes and chose mercenaries and other war profiteers as their villains. But these novels were not propagandistic in the narrow sense of the word. They told of man's inhumanity to man but also of man's altruism, notably his willingness to sacrifice himself for others; in addition to human pettiness, stupidity, duplicity and greed, there were examples of human courage, compassion, and devotion to an ideal. These novelists seemed to be more concerned with comprehending the moral significance of actions taken during a civil war than with blaming the conflict on one side or another. This was a profoundly introspective literature even when attention was focused on surface details of combat and destruction. Themes of madness, terror and social dislocation served to underscore the fragility of human civilizations, particularly when subjected to the kind of irreversible devastation wrought by calculated brutality. In such novels things and people did not fall apart; they were pummeled into oblivion by forces too powerful for them to withstand or else they tried heroically to resist the cataclysmic dehumanization that was overtaking their world. It was not just groups of Africans backed by opposing European factions, not just Biafrans and Federalists, who were in conflict here; good and evil were at war.

Thus, in response to traumatic political and cultural changes since independence, anglophone West African writers have moved from an obsessive concern with the residual effects of colonialism in black Africa to a preoccupation with more universal themes rooted in more specific contemporary realities. In other words, there has been both a narrowing and a broadening of their range of interests. Instead of continuing to delineate the sociological and psychological damage suffered by Africans during the colonial encounter, they attempted to explore dimensions of the human condition by looking more closely at local examples of extreme situations. And they did this primarily through the medium of the novel, an elastic form that can accommodate many different approaches to reality but that has been exploited by these writers in basically two complementary ways: cynical satire (to deal with political corruption) and compassionate realism (to deal with the horrors of civil war). As before, both approaches involved speaking truths plainly so that everyone could easily understand what was being said.

In East Africa, writing got off to a slower start than in West Africa, but production began to accelerate very rapidly in the late 1960s and early 1970s. The first major literary form to emerge was the novel, and in the hands of James Ngugi (now Ngugi wa Thiong'o) and his followers, it initially took essentially the same shape as its counterpart in West Africa. Ngugi's earliest novels, written just before independence, reexamined the colonial past, particularly the period that saw the rise of Gikuyu independent schools and the outbreak of the Mau Mau rebellion. Like Achebe, Ngugi felt that the novelist's work "is often an attempt to come to terms with 'the thing that has been', a struggle, as it were, to sensitively register his encounter with history, his people's history" (1972: 39). The novelists who appeared immediately after Ngugi evidently shared this attitude for they too wrote historical fiction set in the relatively recent past.

Not long after independence, however, East Africa went through the same phase of political disillusionment that had infected West Africa, and novelists responded in the same way by turning their attention to contemporary times. Ngugi's analysis of this phenomenon echoes remarks by Soyinka and Achebe but adds an interesting economic perspective:

> The African writer was in danger of becoming too fascinated by the yesterday of his people and forgetting the present. Involved as he was in correcting his disfigured past, he forgot that his society was no longer peasant, with ownership of means of production, with communal celebration of joy and victory, communal sharing of sorrow and bereavement; his society was no longer organized on egalitarian principles. Conflicts between the emergent elitist middle-class and the masses were developing, their seeds being in the colonial pattern of social and economic development. And when he woke up to his task he was not a little surprised that events in post-independence Africa could take the turn they had taken. (1972: 44-45)

Ngugi was one of the first in East Africa to wake up and write a serious indictment of the turn his nation had taken. He was followed by others who exposed postcolonial political intrigues and social corruption in sharply satirical novels. As in West African fiction, the tendency now was to go beyond blaming Europe for introducing the cultural confusion that culminated in the collapse of modern Africa and begin accusing Africa of collaborating in its own destruction. The critical eye had turned inward.

The other major literary form that emerged in East Africa in the 1960s was the satirical song. In 1966 Okot p'Bitek published *Song of Lawino*, a long "lament" of an illiterate housewife deserted by her educated husband for an emancipated city girl. In registering her complaints against her husband and his "modern woman," Lawino strikes out at the nasty habits and illogical practices of Westernized Africans, contrasting them with the natural dignity of traditional ways. Her song is a hilarious put-down of African "apemanship" (p'Bitek, 1973: 1-5) and a defense of the integrity of indigenous culture, but p'Bitek added interesting piquancy to her argument by making Lawino herself a target of some of the satire. In this manner p'Bitek both revived and undercut the debate about Africa's cultural confusion by placing it in a new comic context. Indeed, he went further and had Lawino's husband reply to her charges in *Song of Ocol*, a book-length lyric in which the technique of reflexive satire is even more pronounced. Unlike the sober-sided West Africans who wrote on such subjects, p'Bitek was ready to laugh at the twisted victims of Africa's collision with Europe. He saw them as sad but funny creatures crushed by a colossal absurdity.

The light touch that p'Bitek introduced into the discussion of heavy cultural issues struck a very responsive chord in East Africa. Imitators immediately sprang up and started singing similar songs. A streak of zany comedy entered the literature, providing a refreshing alternative to the serious indictments of the postcolonial novelists. After p'Bitek the satirical song became one of the most popular literary forms in East Africa.

But it did not remain a static form. In the 1970s singers gradually moved away from cultural to political themes, focusing their attention on some of the same problems preoccupying the novelists. Again p'Bitek led the way, composing in *Song of Prisoner* and *Song of Malaya* eloquent broadsides against a multitude of social and civic sins. The tone of these verbal assaults was still basically humorous, but the humor, particularly in *Song of Prisoner*, now had a bitter aftertaste, reflecting deepened political disillusionment. Also, Europe had vanished; Africa itself was now the epicenter of quaking satire.

Although the literary histories of West and East Africa outlined here are quite similar in certain respects, one significant difference should be underscored: East African writers have had a greater propensity to laugh at evil. While West Africans brood or turn cynical when things go wrong in their society, East Africans seem to have a capacity to enjoy the incongruities of the moment, even when events conspire to work to their disadvantage. Nowhere is this better illustrated than in the popular literature on Idi Amin Dada that emerged in East Africa during and after his tenure as Uganda's Head of State. One of the most interesting specimens of this Idi-otic genre is a beast fable entitled *The Amazing Saga of Field Marshal Abdulla Salim Fisi, or How the Hyena Got His* written by a Ugandan author under the pseudonym "Alumidi Osinya." A brief foreword states:

> The point about the story that follows is that there really is perhaps no better way of talking about the rape of Africa by Africans themselves than the traditional African way of the 'Why' or 'How' animal story. This is how we told off our elders in the past...This is how they told each other off, in a gentle, mild way...Now, perhaps more than ever, when ruthless military dictators are the order of the day and shoot human beings as easily as they shoot the elephants in the National Parks (except that at least with elephants they get the tusks), now really is the time to try the mild, gentle way. Not though, in the Western sense, in the same way the British press, for instance, has regarded our excesses as buffoonery and just laughed them off while we continued needlessly to butcher each other. There is buffoonery, yes, but it's a mirthless, cruel buffoonery and although it may do us good to laugh at ourselves, let our eyes water too: this situation, partly of our own making, is so cruel that we need the sedative of laughter even to be able to look at it. And the effectiveness of the sedative can only be judged by the trickle of tears from the mirthless laughter. (ix-x)

One reason why East African writing differs from West African writing is that East African authors have resorted more often to the sedative of tearful laughter. Even the harshest subjects have been treated in this "mild, gentle way."

Black South African authors, faced with a different set of political circumstances, have produced a literature bearing little resemblance to East or West African writing. Their first major literary form in English was the short story, which flourished in the 1950s but was nearly obliterated in the mid-1960s by tough new censorship legislation. The writers themselves have explained that the pressures of life under apartheid rule, combined with extremely limited opportunities for publication in other forms, made the short story virtually the only literary outlet for "non-white" writers after 1948 (Mphahlele 186; Modisane 3; Nkosi 1962: 6). In the 1950s they wrote either romantic potboilers for *Drum* and other popular home magazines or else hard-hitting naturalistic vignettes for liberal, radical and communist publications. But both this frivolous escapist trash and this serious protest fiction fell victim to the repressive Publications and Entertainments Act of 1963, which gave the South African government power to ban anything it deemed immoral, objectionable or obscene. The most outspoken writers were blacklisted, placed under house arrest, and encouraged to leave South Africa permanently, and the publications that promoted blatant protest writing were quickly forced out of existence. Politically committed writers had to choose between silence and exile.

Those who opted for exile continued to write about South Africa but began to express themselves in a variety of literary forms. Foremost among these was the autobiography, which became the black refugee's favorite medium for articulating his outrage and frustration. Indeed, autobiographical writing almost turned into a tradition among newly exiled black South African intellectuals. Then, having got the experience of apartheid off their chest in this intensely personal way, they experimented with long fiction, drama and various types of poetry, sometimes commenting on the disorientations of exile but usually renewing their attacks on the evils of life back home. Escape from an oppressive environment and release of their long pent-up feelings of bitterness gave them the freedom to explore other modes of getting their message across. They had been liberated from the limitations of the short story.

Meanwhile, back in South Africa the urge for self-expression in English resurfaced in the 1970s in a new literary form—lyric poetry. The poetry movement got started in 1971 with the publication of Oswald Mtshali's *Sounds of a Cowhide Drum*, which sold more than ten thousand copies in its first year. This was followed by increasingly militant books of poetry by others—

Mongane Wally Serote, James Matthews, Sydney Sipho Sepamla, to name only the most prominent. At first the South African censors seemed willing to ignore these poets, possibly because their messages were more obliquely stated than those of the short story writers. Poetry can be more difficult to interpret than prose, and it would have been absurd, even in the South Africa of that day, to have convicted a poet for achieving a splendid ambiguity. What could a court of law do with evidence so slippery as that provided in a transparently simple poem such as "The Notice on the Wall" by Peter Clarke?

> It says clearly on that wall
> "No Ballplaying Allowed."
> But watch this little crowd
> of boys
> Disobey,
> Again today,
> That strict order.
> They give vent
> To one of their
> Great joys
> And kick their muddy ball
> Against that pure-white
> Upright wall. (49)

Oswald Mtshali was equally adept at making a political point through skillful use of irony, as can be seen in his poem "Boy on a Swing."

> Slowly he moves
> to and fro, to and fro
> then faster and faster
> he swishes up and down.
>
> His blue shirt
> billows in the breeze
> like a tattered kite.

The world whirls by:
east becomes west,
north turns to south;
the four cardinal points
meet in his head.

Mother!
Where did I come from?
When will I wear long trousers?
Why was my father jailed? (3)

This is the kind of verse that says things plainly yet indirectly.

However, as more black poetry was published in South Africa, the messages gradually grew cruder and more direct. Instead of carrying figurative titles with subtle political undertones such as *Sounds of a Cowhide Drum* (alluding to the percussive rhythm made by Zulu regiments as they marched into battle beating on their shields) or *Yakhal'inkomo* (the cry of cattle at the slaughter house), the books now had slogans for titles: *Cry Rage!* and *Black Voices Shout!* Soon the government stepped in and started banning such books. The most talented black poets—Mtshali and Serote—left the country for a spell. Thus, in the 1970s history repeated itself in South Africa: a literary movement that gave promise of articulating the discontents of blacks was again halted by heavy-handed government censorship. Black African poets appeared to have no alternative but to remain silent, turn to oral forms, or go into exile. Writing verse in their homeland would make them outlaws.

One significant factor conditioning all African literatures written in African languages has been the audience to whom they have been addressed. In colonial West and East Africa writers tended to speak to Europe first and to their own people second; only after the struggle for independence had been won in principle (if not in fact) did they relax and entertain their countrymen as well as the outside world by laughing at themselves. However as postcolonial disillusionment spread, this laughter turned bitter and self-criticism became the rule. Then African writers spoke primarily to their own people and were no longer greatly concerned about the negative image of Africa their writings might project to outsiders. In this way, East and West African literatures became decidedly more Afrocentric in the postcolonial era.

In South Africa, on the other hand, African authors who expressed themselves in English got their start by writing for popular magazines and newspapers aimed at an indigenous African reading public. Only after leaving South Africa did they concern themselves with writing for a foreign audience; this was more a matter of necessity than preference because as banned persons they could not get their works published or read in their motherland. Those who remained in South Africa continued to speak to their own people until the government made it virtually impossible for them to speak at all.

In black Africa, then, there have been basically two patterns of literary development in European languages since the second world war: the gradual Africanization of literary expression in West and East Africa as colonialism gave way to political self-determination, and the rapid de-Africanization of South African literary expression as repeated repression at home gave rise to a vigorous tradition of protest writing among exiled South Africans abroad. Writers in each area have chosen forms appropriate for conveying a political message to a particular audience and have switched to other forms when environmental conditions have altered. Thus, in morphology as well as ideology, literary art has been responsive to the winds of change that swept across sub-Saharan Africa in the mid-twentieth century. The intellectual history of a continent undergoing rapid cultural transformation can be discerned in the significant mutations such literatures manifest.

Xenophobia and Class Consciousness in African Writing

African literatures in non-African languages are in essence a paradox, an aberration, a twentieth-century cultural anomaly requiring explanation. How did such unusual literatures come into being? What prompted the first authors to express themselves in foreign tongues? To whom were they addressing their messages? What did they wish to communicate? Why did they bother to write poetry, fiction or drama at all?

One answer to this cluster of riddles is that such literatures originated as responses to European racism, particularly the kind of racism that assumed Africans to be inferior creatures incapable of high civilization. What better way to prove the colonial master wrong than to sing impressively in his own tongue, to engage him in intellectual debate? What better way to assert one's own humanity and demand the respect due to an equal? The impulse toward heightened self-expression in European languages was therefore not a self-indulgent outpouring of private, elitist emotion but rather a calculated assault on European sensibilities, using the best weapons available in the struggle for wide public recognition of the legitimacy of Africa's claims to human brotherhood. African literatures thus reinforced the political argument that Africans should be in control of their own future, should rule themselves. In this sense Africa's earliest authors could be said to have produced anticolonial propaganda. Their ambition was to subvert European notions of preordained supremacy.

The strategies adopted by the first major francophone and anglophone authors differed, as did the political realities they had to confront. The francophones, led by Léopold Sédar Senghor, countered French cultural hegemony by formulating a philosophy of self-affirmation which they called Negritude. To the French who said, "You are different from us until you have fully assimilated our language and culture and then can be accepted, at least in theory, as equals," the Negritudinists replied, "Yes, we are different, and *vive la différence!* Even our French education makes us no less African and our Africanness no less equal." Senghor conceptualized the racial difference as one of innate propensity: Europe is Reason, Africa Emotion. Thus, to the Cartesian syllogism, "I think, therefore I am," he appended an African corollary: "I feel, therefore I too am." Senghor's definition of Negritude as "the sum total of the cultural values of Africa" (99) placed emphasis on what he considered a distinctive way of life, one sufficiently different from others as to constitute a separate but not inferior mode of being. Africa's contribution to world civilization would be its warm humanism, which contrasted sharply with Europe's cold rationality. Some have characterized such ideas as a form of "anti-racist racism" (Sartre), but it is possible to see them as a riposte with a much deeper significance, for by turning a presumed liability (i.e., Africa's difference from Europe) into a positive asset, Negritude challenged Western cultural arrogance at its weakest point—not its insistence on racial difference but its bland assumption of cultural superiority. By conceding the first point, one could more powerfully contest the second. Negritude, far from being a negative movement, gave Africa a wholesome new identity.

The anglophone writers, in the meantime, were up against a different kind of racism so they adopted other tactics. The British attitude toward Africans has frequently been characterized as standoffish. Unlike the French, they seemed to be saying to their colonial subjects, "You are different from us, and even after you have fully assimilated our language and culture, you cannot be accepted, even in theory, as equals." To this the anglophone writers replied, "We too are civilized members of the human community, and you have no right to deny our humanity or equality." To prove their point, they wrote about the African past, showing how African civilizations functioned before Europeans arrived on the scene. Chinua Achebe, whose novels defined this genre of historical fiction, summed up his own approach in the following words:

> One big message, of the many that I try to put across, is that Africa was not a vacuum before the coming of Europe, that culture was not unknown in Africa, that culture was not brought to Africa by the white world. You would have thought it was obvious that everybody had a past, but there were people who came to Africa and said, "You have no history, you have no civilization, you have no culture, you have no religion. You are lucky we are here. Now you are hearing about these things from us for the first time." Well, you know, we didn't just drop from the sky. We too had our own history, traditions, cultures, civilizations. It is not possible for one culture to come to another and say, "I am the way, the truth, and the life; there is nothing else but me." If you say this, you are guilty of irreverence or arrogance. You are also stupid. And this is really my concern. (Lindfors, et al 7)

So Achebe's interest in correcting colonial stupidity led him to present a dignified image of the African past, an image that undercut European stereotypes of the "Dark Continent." But though his mission, like Senghor's, was to affirm the integrity of African civilization, he proceeded by emphasizing commonalities, not differences, in human beings from dissimilar societies. Africans were no worse and no better than Europeans, for they all were members of the same species, sharing the virtues and faults characteristic of every one of their kind.

Anglophone authors have been rather unsympathetic—indeed, sometimes even hostile to Negritude. Their reactions have ranged from humorous quips such as Wole Soyinka's famous observation that "A tiger does not [have to] proclaim his tigritude" (quoted in Jahn 1966: 265) to more impatient outbursts such as Es'kia Mphahlele's denunciation of the whole concept of a distinctive African personality (1965: 22-26). The uniformly negative response of black South African writers can be traced to their own peculiar political environment, for the white South African regime, for reasons of its own, was eager to perpetuate the notion that people of different races are basically unequal and incompatible and therefore need to be kept apart. This was the ideology underlying apartheid, a policy meant to separate the races. Black South African writers, faced with brutal daily reminders of their country's institutionalized racism, therefore rejected any suggestion that Africans were fundamentally unlike other peoples, for this was precisely the kind of thinking that the South African government had been trying to force upon them. For sound ideological reasons they opposed racism of any sort—even "anti-racist racism."

The battle, then, in West, East and South, initially took the form of seeking a definition of self and society that would contradict prevailing Western notions about the backwardness of African peoples. By creating bright new images, African literatures in European languages helped to shape and reify concepts of group identity that served to unite disparate African ethnic groups into cohesive political units that could effectively oppose European domination of the continent. Negritude and other forms of self-affirmation thus accelerated the process of decolonization in Africa by giving Africans a fresh vision of themselves and their history. Writers contributed to the nationalist struggle by liberating the minds of their countrymen.

But after independence the nature of the African political struggle changed and so did the focus of African writing. As African leaders took over the reins of power and started making decisions that inevitably alienated some of their followers, the unity that had been achieved during the nationalist crusade began to crumble and disharmonies became more evident. Fragile new democracies found themselves plagued by economic instability, social unrest, bureaucratic inefficiency and widespread corruption. Politicians were now perceived not as self-sacrificing heroes but as self-serving villains and rogues who took no interest in discharging their duties and safeguarding the welfare of the public unless they could enrich themselves at the same time (Lindfors 1969). A mood of profound disillusionment set in, reflected in a rash of satirical novels and plays that heaped scorn on Africa's new ruling class. Achebe explained his own reorientation during this period as a consequence of political disenchantment:

> Having fought with the nationalist movements and been on the side of the politicians, I realized after independence that they and I were now on different sides, because they were not doing what we had agreed they should do. So I had to become a critic. I found myself on the side of the people against their leaders—leaders this time being black people. I was still doing my job as a writer, but one aspect of the job had changed. I think what you do as a writer depends on the state of your society. (Lindfors et al 8)

When the state of African society subsequently underwent another change—this time from democracy to military rule—writers responded by attacking tyranny and ruthless dictatorship. Soldiers replaced politicians as the primary targets of ridicule. However, since it was difficult in some countries to express such ideas openly without risking imprisonment, torture or even death, the writers who chose to protest had to resort to subtle symbolic techniques or else launch their arrows from abroad. Serumaga in Uganda turned to wordless pantomime, Soyinka castigated foreign or fallen megalomaniacs, others wrote beast fables and mock epics, sometimes publishing them in exile or withholding them from publication until a new regime took over. Several well-known authors appear to have stopped writing altogether, perhaps preferring silence to loud censure. For the politically aware, pessimism became the dominant idiom of creative discourse. The world was an evil place, and many of the most active devils were Africans. The paradise that political independence was supposed to have ushered in now seemed unattainable. Africa had lost its innocence, and Africans themselves were largely to blame.

But the role of Satan in this modern melodrama remained reserved for foreign actors, mainly Europeans and Americans who as agents of cold war politics or international capitalism sought to undermine the stability of African states and compromise the integrity of African leaders by offering temptations too attractive to resist. The West was presumed to have a vested interest in the collapse of African political institutions, in the corruption and venality of African leadership. A strain of xenophobia entered postcolonial African literature, with some of the continent's most illustrious authors as its principal carriers. One could see it as a vague shadow in Achebe's *A Man of the People*, where British Amalgamated as well as American and East European interests lurk in the background of the narrative, contributing cash and courtesies to competing political parties in an effort to manipulate them. Chief Nanga himself, the arch-villain of the novel, openly accepts bribes for his services. His rivals, a more ethical sort, debate the merits of following suit, even though they have a few scruples about using such money in a manner not intended by the briber. Clearly this is a political arena that has been polluted by contact with foreign moneybags. Even the good guys are morally confused.

Xenophobia can be seen in much starker terms in the works of two of Africa's most prolific writers: Ayi Kwei Armah and Ngugi wa Thiong'o. Armah, who began his career as one of the disillusioned authors of the 1960s, used his first novel, *The Beautyful Ones Are Not Yet Born*, to attack social and political corruption in postcolonial Ghana. It is a memorable tale, told with a connoisseur's eye for visceral details that vividly convey the stench and flavor of every conceivable kind of decay. Yet this excremental vision of Nkrumah's Ghana is not wholly original, for it is informed by Fanonist ideas that seek to explain the all-encompassing rot in postcolonial societies as a natural by-product of ex-colonial people's perverse lingering love for their former colonizer. The slant can be seen in passages such as the following:

There is something so terrible in watching a black man trying at all points to be the dark ghost of a European, and that was what we were seeing in those days. Men who had risen to lead the hungry came in clothes they might have been hoping to use at Governors' Balls on the birthday of the white people's queen, carrying cuff links that shone insultingly in the faces of men who had stolen pennies from their friends. They came late and spoke to their servants in the legal English they had spent their lives struggling to imitate, talking of constitutions and offering us unseen ghosts of words and paper held holy by Europeans, and they asked us to be faithful and to trust in them. They spoke to us in the knowledge that they were our magicians, people with some secret power behind them. They were not able in the end to understand the people's unbelief. How could they understand that even those who have not been anywhere know that the black man who has spent his life fleeing from himself into whiteness has no power if the white master gives him none? How were these leaders to know that while they were climbing up to shit in their people's faces, their people had seen their arseholes and drawn away in disgusted laughter? (95-96)

Armah, like Achebe, vigorously attacks African political leaders here, but he too sees them as men corrupted by their contact with the West. They are men who have lost their African identity through striving to become carbon copies of the white men who formerly ruled them. Love of the West thus leads to the death of Africa.

Armah's subsequent novels have carried this theme further. For example, in *Why Are We So Blest?* there is a ritual castration scene in which the blood of an emblematic African male is consumed by an emblematic American female. In *Two Thousand Seasons* Arabs (who are called "predators") and Europeans (who are called "destroyers") are shown to be responsible for converting Africa from a place of gentleness, peace and tranquillity to a place of chaos and violence; Armah's message is that Africans must avenge these wrongs by exterminating the predators and destroying the destroyers. Here xenophobia is taken to its ultimate extreme. Armah goes beyond "anti-racist racism" to a racially selective misanthropy. Rather like Hitler, he wants his homeland to return to a state of mythical ancestral racial purity. Paradise must be all black.

Ngugi wa Thiong'o's xenophobia is of a different sort. He is not afraid of people but of an economic system that oppresses Africans, making them subservient to Western interests. He places his faith not in politicians, landowners or other representatives of the overprivileged African elite but in the masses—the ordinary peasants and workers who, he hopes, will one day rise up and overthrow their oppressors, establishing a more equitable economic system in the process. He is not a misanthrope but a Marxist.

Ngugi has not always held radical ideas. Indeed, his early novels, short stories and journalistic pieces are quite free of the socioeconomic jargon that colors his more recent works. He started as an ardent nationalist, following in Achebe's footsteps by recreating Kenya's colonial past in an effort to make his countrymen aware of what they had lost *and gained* in their initial encounters with the West. After independence he went through a period of political disenchantment, which was given its fullest expression in his third novel, *A Grain of Wheat*. It was not until the late 1970s that he began taking a more doctrinaire line and putting his new social ideas into fictional form. The turning point was his fourth novel, *Petals of Blood*, published in 1977 but written over a six-year span in three countries—the United States, Kenya and the Soviet Union. One need only quote a passage from the last pages of this novel to capture the tenor of Ngugi's argument:

> Imperialism: capitalism: landlords: earthworms. A system that bred hordes of round-bellied jiggers and bedbugs with parasitism and cannibalism as the highest goal in society. This system and its profiteering gods and its ministering angels had hounded [Karega's] mother to her grave. These parasites would always demand the sacrifice of blood from the working masses. These few who had prostituted the whole land turning it over to foreigners

for thorough exploitation, would drink people's blood and say hypocritical prayers of devotion to skin oneness and to nationalism even as skeletons of bones walked to lonely graves. The system and its gods and its angels had to be fought consciously, consistently and resolutely by all the working people! From Koitalel through Kang'ethe to Kimathi it had been the peasants, aided by the workers, small traders and small landowners, who had mapped out the path. Tomorrow it would be the workers and the peasants leading the struggle and seizing power to overturn the system of all its preying bloodthirsty gods and gnomic angels, bringing to an end the reign of the few over the many and the era of drinking blood and feasting on human flesh. Then, only then, would the kingdom of man and woman really begin, they joying and loving in creative labour. (344)

So paradise, for Ngugi, starts with a proletarian revolution and a restructuring of the economy. Western imperialism must be resisted and destroyed so Kenyans can enter a brave, new "kingdom of man and woman."

After *Petals of Blood* was finished, Ngugi attempted to disseminate his views more widely by addressing Kenyan peasants and workers more directly. This he did by co-authoring a play in his mother-tongue, Gikuyu, for performance by working-class people at a literacy center in his hometown, Limuru. The play was performed for seven weeks in October and November of 1977 before being closed down by Kenyan authorities who branded it "provocative" and "not to the best interest of the republic in general" (Mungai wa Kamau). Forty days later Ngugi was picked up by the police for questioning, and he was not released until nearly a year later. He spent almost all of 1978 in detention without any formal charges ever being filed against him.

The play, entitled *Ngaahika Ndeenda* (I will marry when I want), was built around a triple theme of economic, religious and sexual exploitation. Kiguunda, a poor farm laborer, is persuaded by Kioi, his wealthy Christian employer, to sanctify his "sinful" traditional marriage in church. Kiguunda does not have enough money to pay for the expensive ceremony so he borrows some from Kioi's bank by offering his own one-and-a-half acres of farm land as collateral. When he defaults on the loan, the land is auctioned off and Kioi buys it so that he and a business associate can build an insecticide factory on it in partnership with a foreign firm. While this is going on, Kioi's playboy son seduces and impregnates Kiguunda's daughter and then rejects her. Kiguunda confronts Kioi on this issue, but Kioi denies that his son would have taken up with a "prostitute" and challenges Kiguunda to bring the matter to court so that "we shall see on whose side the law is" (101). Kiguunda responds by drawing his sword and threatening Kioi's life, a gesture that could be interpreted as symbolizing the successful armed revolt of the exploited masses against their bourgeois oppressors.

The play itself was not banned by the authorities. Rather, the District Commissioner revoked the Kamirithu Centre's license to perform it. The play was published in Gikuyu by Heinemann East Africa in April 1980 and sold quite briskly, going through three printings (a total of 13,000 copies) in its first three months on the market. The Kenyan government had not attempted to prevent or discourage its publication or to interfere with its distribution to booksellers—facts that would seem to confirm the notion that oral performances speak louder than printed words in Kenya.

Why should a rural production of *Ngaahika Ndeenda* have been found so objectionable as to necessitate government suppression? After all, the play itself was not directly critical of the government nor was it unpopular locally. Indeed, according to reports in the newspapers, this three-hour musical drama was an extraordinarily successful show, and people were coming from miles around to see it. Moreover, it was a community enterprise, almost a model *harambee* (self-help) project that involved a cross-section of the Limuru population—peasants, factory workers, petty traders, unemployed youths, university lecturers. It had originated as a scheme to promote and sustain literacy among villagers who had been taught to read and write at the Kamirithu

Community Educational and Cultural Centre. Ngugi wa Mirii, who was supervising these literacy classes, and Ngugi wa Thiong'o, who was living in the community while teaching at the University of Nairobi, had been commissioned by the governing committee of the Centre to write a play that would give the new literates in the community something to do that would help them improve their recently acquired skills. The villagers actually collaborated in the development of the script, designed and built the open-air theater, and raised the 75,000 shillings (about $10,000) necessary to produce the play . From start to finish, the production was truly a communal undertaking.

What appears to have worried the authorities was the play's immense popularity. Had it been a flop or fiasco, the government probably would not have bothered to intervene, preferring instead to allow this unusual theatrical experiment to die a quick, natural death. But the play was attracting hordes of viewers, the vast majority of whom were unrestrainedly enthusiastic about what they saw.

And it wasn't only the spectacle of a vibrant stage performance involving singing, dancing and drama that enthralled them; the message embedded in the play was getting across. Ngugi himself has said:

> I believe that the play, *Ngaahika Ndeenda*, was very popular because it talked about the extreme poverty of the people. I believe the play was popular because it talked about landlessness in our country. I believe the play was popular because it talked about the betrayal of the peasants and workers by the political "big-wigs". I believe the play was popular because it talked about the arrogance and the greed of the powerful and the wealthy. Again, I believe the play was popular because it depicted the true conditions of the rural people in the rural villages. (Gacheru 32)

If all this is so, then it is not surprising that the District Commissioner of Kiambu received complaints about the performance from some members of the community who did not approve of what was being said and enacted on the Kamirithu stage. These complaints, supplemented by eye-witness reports from his officers, led the D.C. to decide to shut down the play, even though he himself had never seen a performance.

The reasons given by the Kiambu D.C. for taking this course of action are worth scrutinizing (see Mungai wa Kamau and Munene). In elaborating his charge that the production was "provocative," the D.C. reiterated some of the complaints he had received that "the songs, dances and even the dialogue in the play were aimed at creating conflict between different classes of people in Kenya." He noted in particular that the term "homeguards" (kamatimu) had been used frequently and that "such terms should not be used in public or elsewhere, since they could in the long run revive the bitterness of the Emergency period." Further, he felt that the play sought to "urge people to engage in a 'free-or-all' class war." He concluded his remarks by repeating that "the play does not put across the idea of reminding people to forget the past as our good government has been exhorting us."

These are far from trivial issues in the Gikuyu highlands, an area bloodied by very bitter fighting during the Mau Mau war. There are still many old wounds from that war that have not healed with time, many old scores that have never been settled. The play, the D.C. was saying, was reviving past animosities, reopening those wounds. The issue of "homeguards" was a particularly sensitive one, for this was the term applied to the Gikuyu who had fought in the war for independence on the side of the British colonial government. Some of these "homeguards" were portrayed in the play as among the worst of Kenya's neocolonial exploiters today, men who had profited handsomely from the national independence they had earlier sought to forestall, retard or subvert. The D.C. apparently feared that the play, by stirring up memories of the past, might lead to a disturbance of the peace, perhaps even to serious violence and mayhem. The revocation of the license of the play may therefore be viewed as an effort to maintain law and order by suppressing a reawakening of the community's collective consciousness of history.

But the detention of Ngugi wa Thiong'o forty days later must be regarded as an act of another sort, especially since he was never charged with any crimes. It appears that he was victimized both as a penalty for his writings and as a warning to others who might be tempted by his example to mix too much politics with literature. Since no one else associated with *Ngaahika Ndeenda*—his co-author, the director, the actors—was detained, one must conclude that it was not the play alone that led to Ngugi's imprisonment; the play may have been the last straw but it was not the only straw in Ngugi's case. Also, since no charges were filed against him, it must be assumed that the Kenyan government knew that it had no legal justification for denying him his freedom. The state was deliberately victimizing him for no valid juridical reason. So while the closing down of the play may be seen as a preventive measure, the detention of Ngugi must be recognized as a terror tactic.

This lesson was not lost on Ngugi, who immediately resolved to write all his future creative works in Gikuyu. In fact, during his year in detention he completed an allegorical novel, *Caitaani Mutharaba-Ini*, which he subsequently translated and published in English under the title *Devil on the Cross*. Since his release he has written in Gikuyu at least one more play, three children's books and another novel. It is conceivable that he would have written even more had he been able to remain in Kenya. However, for a variety of reasons he lives in exile today, cut off— physically at least—from the audience he most ardently wants to address. His books continue to circulate in Kenya, but the plays are not performed and the novels and children's books do not appear on school reading lists. Writing in Gikuyu has not given him the platform he had hoped to secure.

Ngugi's situation has been discussed at some length because he is one of the few writers in Africa who has quite deliberately sought to cultivate a new audience by writing in an African language rather than a European one. Moreover, he has attempted to reach illiterate and semi-literate people by writing for the stage rather than for the page. Unlike any of his peers who have won an equal measure of international fame by writing in English, he has turned in a totally new direction, heedless of rather dire personal consequences. He has said publicly that he would rather communicate with a single peasant in Kenya than with ten thousand readers overseas (reported by Bentsi-Enchill). He is therefore a phenomenon of unusual significance on the African literary scene.

But he is a lonely phenomenon and one whose fate is not likely to inspire others to emulate him. Who else would be willing to give up so much—family, friends and financial security, to name just a few—to pursue such a principle? There are other African writers living in exile today, but how many of them got into difficulty with authorities at home by switching their language of literary expression? In anglophone Africa Ngugi may be unique, and he may well remain unique. He is a man without a country because he tried to take his message to the countryside. He tried to speak to the victims of the economic system he deplored, not to its beneficiaries.

Modern African literatures in European languages have seldom been concerned directly and exclusively with the lot of the common man. They have not sought to approach Africa's problems at a grassroots level. Indeed, they have rarely condescended to address themselves to the lower classes, to peasants and workers. Rather, they have been preoccupied primarily with the problems of the educated elite, the large and small traumas of those who have been schooled in Western languages, Western manners, Western ideas. It is no surprise, then, that initially they were obsessively concerned with commenting on Africa's relationship with Europe, for who could be more conscious of European racism and the manifold consequences of European colonialism than those Africans who were at the top and therefore were most immediately impacted by policies based on racial discrimination and political domination? And after the winds of change had swept across the continent unfurling dozens of new flags, who but the still powerless elite would be likely to voice so quickly so much disappointment in the leaders that the unwashed masses had elected to rule the country? The soldiers were simply much more deadly rivals for power, winning their new positions with bullets instead of ballots; it was prudent to criticize them from a safe distance—geographically or linguistically.

But the easiest course of all was to reopen the dialogue with the West, using paradigms and conventions learned in and out of school to blame much of the postcolonial mess on new forms of Western colonialism that relied on the collaboration or collusion of corrupted Africans. Paradise had been lost through colonialism, but optimists who believed in the inevitability of revolution felt confident it could be regained through the eradication of neocolonialism. Only Ngugi saw that this new struggle would require abandoning one's loyalty to the instrument that had made the older struggles effective: one would have to begin to speak in a language that ordinary people could comprehend. Until that happens on a much broader scale, African literatures will continue to face West and concern themselves narcissistically with the indentity crises of the mandarins.

xile and Aesthetic Distance in the
Works of Peter Abrahams

In *Return to Goli* (1953), an autobiographical account of his first
visit to his native land after fourteen years spent in voluntary
exile, Peter Abrahams wrote:

> In 1939 I had signed on a ship as stoker and left South Africa. I had
> come away charged with bitterness against the whites of that land
> in particular and all whites in general. Life there had allowed me
> no self-respect, no dignity. And I had left suffering from a colossal
> inferiority complex, and carrying a huge chip on my shoulder. Life
> in that country had made me humourless, intense and bitter. Also,
> because I had protested against things as they were, I had not been
> able to earn a living...
>
> But my spiritual and emotional want, much more than my
> physical want, had been the driving motive behind my leaving the
> land of my birth. The need to be psychologically free of the colour
> bar had, over the years, grown into a kind of obsession, blinding
> as all obsessions are. And in that year my obsession with this need
> had reached breaking point. I had to escape or slip into that negative
> destructiveness that is the offspring of bitterness and frustration.
>
> I had escaped and reached England at the end of 1941 after
> two years at sea...England had been kind to me. It had given me
> the chance to build a decent dignified life for myself. In it I had
> learnt to laugh and play, and found my love. It had given me access
> to forms of beauty. Its climate of mental freedom had allowed me
> to pursue my thoughts as far as they would go, and without fear.
> And I had made true friendships there...
>
> [But] I am a child of the plural societies. When the strains and
> pressures had grown too much for me, I had escaped from the

physical presence of the problem [of racial antagonism]. But the problem itself is inescapable. It will be with me either till it is resolved or till the end of my days. It is the raw material of my work. The most challenging, the most exciting raw material in the world—and also, in one sense, the most inhibiting. (13-15, 17, 29)

At the time he made this statement, Abrahams, though only thirty-four years old, had already earned an international reputation as a writer, having published a volume of short stories and four novels since his arrival in England. All these works— *Dark Testament* (1942), *Song of the City* (1945), *Mine Boy* (1946), *The Path of Thunder* (1948), and *Wild Conquest* (1950)—focused entirely on problems in South Africa. Not one dealt with experiences elsewhere in the world, even though Abrahams by the end of the Second World War had lived most of his adult life abroad. England may have been his adopted haven, the place where he felt free enough emotionally to pursue his ambition to write, but South Africa remained his true home, dominating his imagination and channeling his creative energy toward expressions of protest in fiction. Geographically he was in exile, but spiritually he was still a child of his motherland, a sad, moody, sentimental lad lost in homesick reveries.

Perhaps it was his emotional ambivalence toward South Africa, his confused feelings of love and hate, that led to some of the failures in his early fiction. He seemed so determined to prove that sensitive human beings could transcend ethnic differences and effect a meaningful union that he could not refrain from orchestrating mawkish love affairs and resorting to clichés of class struggle. He dealt too readily in stereotypes, giving characters quasi-allegorical dimensions as cardboard embodiments of abstract ideas. He blended violence with sentiment, producing overblown melodrama laced with bathos. Plot gave way to undisciplined passion, narrative development to didacticism. Yet amid the untidiest clutter of unhappy incidents and ugly denouements Abrahams somehow always managed to maintain a serene optimism about the future. His fiction seemed to promise that in the end, things would turn out all right. The world would someday be a better place. Progress, real human progress, ultimately would be made. Even his darkest tragic stories had this kind of subliminal silver lining. Love and hate. Hate yet redemptive love. Aeschylus may have had optimists like Peter Abrahams in mind when he said, "I know how men in exile feed on dreams" (77: 1. 1668).

Abrahams himself was conscious that he might be living in a dream world and wondered whether the "tolerant and humanistic view of life" he had developed in the tranquillity of exile was "a true view":

> Was it really mine? Could it stand the strains and stresses of life in South Africa, or, indeed, in any of the other plural societies of East and Central Africa?
> There was no way of knowing except by going there. My faith had to be tested on the battlefield of race hatred. Only thus could I be certain. (27-28)

So in 1952, four years after the Nationalist Party had come to power in South Africa and five years before the Gold Coast became independent Ghana, Abrahams returned to South Africa for six weeks as a reporter for the London *Observer*. He also visited Kenya for a week before going back to London. *Return to Goli* records his impressions of what was happening at that time in two corners of white-ruled Africa.

Abrahams's fact-finding mission had an immediate impact on his imaginative writing. After completing the book of reportage, he went on to write *Tell Freedom* (1954), an autobiography recounting his youth and adolescence in South Africa up to the very day he boarded the stoker and started his life in exile. Obviously the trip home had brought back a flood of memories, and these he set down with a novelist's flair for telling detail. The first half of *Tell Freedom* contains some of Abrahams's finest writing—vivid vignettes of slum life seen from the perspective of a child growing up and learning the lessons such an environment has to teach. More evocative than any other book he has written, it focuses on the deprivations that are part of the daily life of "non-whites" in a racially divided society. Even today, nearly half a century later, it remains a very moving book and one of the best examples of nostalgic autobiographical writing by a South African in exile. Abrahams's homecoming, by putting him back in direct contact with his roots, had a very beneficial effect on his art. It enabled him to rediscover the stark realities of the landscape he had left behind He was no longer adrift in the shadows of an alien dream world.

His next book was also a stunner, but its power derived not from a fidelity to the texture of South African experience but rather from an agility at placing South African problems in a larger continental context. It was as if Abrahams, after looking at his world through a microscope, had drawn back to view it through a different set of lenses that permitted him to perceive its relationship to the rest of the globe. A Wreath for Udomo (1956) was a novel set mainly in tropical Africa, most of the action taking place in a country called Panafrica, where an archetypal nationalist, Michael Udomo, was leading the struggle for political independence. Udomo, clearly modeled on Kwame Nkrumah, Jomo Kenyatta, Nnamdi Azikiwe and other prominent nationalist politicians in West and East Africa, managed to win self-determination for Panafrica by marshaling mass support for his cause, but on becoming head of state, he began to alienate some of his followers by making decisions they found objectionable. His ambition was to hurry his people into the twentieth century by industrializing and Westernizing Panafrica as quickly as possible so that it would be transformed into a modern, self-sufficient nation-state that could serve as a model of progress for all of Africa. To have a chance of attaining this goal, Udomo found it necessary to betray one of his best friends, David Mhendi, who was engaged in a guerrilla war to liberate white-ruled Pluralia, Panafrica's neighbor to the south. In other words, Udomo, when faced with the choice between developing his own newly independent country or assisting in the struggle for political freedom elsewhere in the continent, elected to put his own people and his own goals first. And by doing so, he stirred up the kind of internal opposition in Panafrica that soon led to his downfall. At the end of the novel he is massacred in a bloody ritual by reactionary comrades who had earlier supported him, but Abrahams suggests that the social revolution Udomo had set in motion could not now be halted. Udomo's death was only a temporary setback; his visionary ambitions for Panafrica were destined to be realized.

What made *A Wreath for Udomo* controversial was its topicality in 1956, only a year before the Gold Coast was to become the first tropical African nation to complete the process of decolonization. The first half of the novel could be recognized as a transcription of the nationalist era, when charismatic African leaders gained popular backing and successfully challenged colonial regimes, forcing them to yield political power. But the second half of the novel, the part set in independent Panafrica, was a projection into the future, and African readers were shocked to find Abrahams predicting doom for the nationalists after independence. Wasn't this a rather gloomy view of what the next few years would bring? Yet Abrahams had constructed his scenario carefully, basing the final conflicts in the novel on the tensions he perceived between new nation-building aspirations in the tropics and continuing revolutionary struggles in the south. Would Africa's first Prime Ministers and Presidents sell out someone else's revolution in order to attempt to work economic miracles at home? Abrahams evidently felt they would, and he applauded both their courage and their convictions. In his view material prosperity was more valuable to Africa than political solidarity, for the real revolution would be brought about by modernization and Westernization. Udomo, he hinted, did not die in vain, for others would surely carry on the transformational mission that had earned him martyrdom. This ambitious nation-builder was the kind of visionary leader who had charted a new direction for Africa by leading it away from the indigenous evils of its past. Udomo was a fallen hero who deserved a wreath.

This was a strange story for a South African writer to tell, but perhaps it is not so surprising that Peter Abrahams told it, for by this time he must have been acutely aware that he could no longer claim to be a South African writer. He was from that place, but he was no longer of that place. His seventeen years in exile had made him a different person, and South Africa itself had changed. His visit in 1952 had refreshed his memory of his early years there, but he must have felt out of his element in a political environment he could no longer recognize or embrace as home. By now he was a citizen of a much larger world, and the attitudes expressed in his writing reflected an awareness of international dimensions of human conflict. He was writing not just about Johannesburg, Cape Town, Natal or the northern Karroo but about a wider arena of experience in which South Africa figured somewhere out at the periphery, not right at the center. His homecoming may have made him realize how far he had grown away from the land that previously had been his single source of creative inspiration. He may have seen that he was now distanced from South Africa by more than geography. Indeed, he was detached from it intellectually, emotionally, and therefore also aesthetically. He could be more objective about his homeland because he had been away from it so long that he had developed a wider network of allegiances. South Africa had become only one of his many concerns. He was now committed to the whole of Africa, not merely to its southernmost extremity.

And soon his commitment was to extend even farther. In 1955 he traveled to Jamaica to write a book about that island for the Corona Library, "a series of illustrated volumes under the sponsorship of the Colonial Office dealing with the United Kingdom's dependent territories, the way their peoples live, and how they are governed" (Abrahams, *Jamaica* v) But no sooner had he delivered the manuscript of *Jamaica: An Island Mosaic* (1957) to the Colonial Office than he "felt the pull of this sunny island once more" and decided to return there to live (xiii).

Abrahams still resides in Kingston today, having remained there longer than he had lived in either South Africa or England. What attracted him most to this new environment can be found in the last pages of his book about Jamaica:

> I had been born and brought up in a multi-racial society where the present was ugly and the future promised to be uglier. There the problems of race and colour, perhaps the key problems of our century, were so riddled with fear and hate that they seemed beyond any but the most terrible and bloody solution.
>
> In Jamaica, and in my exploring of its past and its problems, I had seen the solution of that problem. The Jamaicans had lived out the multi-racial problem and were now reaching a stage where race and colour did not matter, only a person's worth as a person. In this they are far ahead of most of the rest of the world; have much to teach the rest of the world. (260-61)

So Abrahams chose to relocate himself and his family in a multi-racial society as different from South Africa as possible. He was seeking a color-blind exile.

Following the move, Abrahams was silent for some time. When his next novel, *A Night of Their Own*, surfaced in 1965, it seemed to mark a regression to an earlier phase in his writing career, for it dealt exclusively with South Africa and told an improbable story overwrought with melodrama, clichés and stereotypes. This time the focus was on the involvement of Indians in Natal in an underground movement threatened by internecine racial frictions but simultaneously raised to new heights of social awareness via miscegenated love affairs. It was the old love/hate dichotomy again, played out against a backdrop of oppression, attempted subversion, and heavy-breathing romance. But the artificiality of the drama, exacerbated by unrelenting emblematic use of character and incident, showed just how far out of touch Abrahams was with real events in post-Sharpeville South Africa. The novel may be read as a simple adventure story or as a moral fable but not as a convincing slice of revolutionary life, which may be what it was meant to have been.

The next year Abrahams's first novel about his new environment was published. In *This Island Now* (1966) Abrahams transferred his preoccupation with political and racial themes to the Caribbean, where a power struggle was shown to be in progress. A popular politician, on assuming the presidency of an independent island state, tried to give the poor, downtrodden black masses a greater say in government, but in order to do this, he had to take away some of the advantages that privileged whites, foreign and indigenous, continued to enjoy. The major conflicts in the novel were in fact based mainly on color and class, which seems more than a little surprising considering Abrahams's earlier effusions about color-blindness in Jamaica. Had his experiences living in the Caribbean changed his perspective on racial realities there, or was he, as a transplanted South African with a lifetime of practice in viewing the world in black and white terms, predisposed to discover color prejudice as the root of all evil wherever he went? Was he genuinely disillusioned or was he destined to grow disgruntled as a result of always wearing race-tinted glasses? In any case, the novel was an artistic failure because it exhibited the same excesses as his earlier explorations of racial politics in his native land. Was South Africa, even at this temporal, geographical and aesthetic distance, still ruining his art?[1]

Unfortunately, these questions must be raised again when we examine his latest and longest novel, *The View from Coyaba* (1985), published nearly two decades after *This Island Now*. One has the feeling that Abrahams tried to distill in this novel a lifetime of thinking about what has often been termed "the black experience." The book attempts a kaleidoscopic view of about 150 years of black history in the Caribbean, North America and tropical Africa, following the fortunes of successive generations in a single family who are exposed to archetypal as well as actual historical happenings in their quest for a better life. The time scheme is broad enough to cover everything from early nineteenth-century slave revolts in the Caribbean to the atrocities of Idi Amin in Uganda, and there is even a brief prelude depicting Arawak resistance to the Spaniards in sixteenth-century Jamaica, an episode that sets the tone for the saga of collective racial struggle that follows. Some isolated moments in this vast sweep of experience are captured memorably, but because Abrahams must strain to provide credible continuity between events located in distant pockets of space and time, he cannot wholly resist the temptation to bend his characters into awkward rhetorical postures so that they can be used to ventilate all the important ideological issues of their day and at the same time advance the plot to the next family crisis occasioned by documented racial calamity. As a strategy of narration this was a juggling act of heroic proportions—indeed, of hubristic proportions, for some of the many weighty spheres placed in motion were bound to fall flat, bounce wildly, and spoil the effect of this grand spectacle. The novel was simply too ambitious for its own good.

But the biggest disappointment derived not from the novel's structure or design but from its message, which was one of black separatism, of black withdrawal from engagement with the West. To survive as a people, blacks, it was maintained, must rely solely on themselves. Abrahams had his major surviving character state in the closing pages of the novel that

> One of the most terrible things about the Westernism from which we must withdraw to find ourselves is its loss of faith and direction, of the capacity to know, instinctively, the true imperatives for historical survival. To be of any use to ourselves...we must separate ourselves from this destructive Westernism...If we succeed we may free ourselves in time to point to a new way of seeing our world, a new way of living with each other and understanding each other; we may all learn to co-operate instead of compete, to share instead of grab...A healed people, a whole people, freed of the bitter historical scars, may have something rich to offer the world. (437, 439-40)

The black utopia toward which this character was groping, the paradise of health and wholesomeness that Abrahams was advocating through him, would require not just withdrawal from the West but also the establishment of a form of global apartheid. One is forced to conclude that almost a half a century of exile had finally turned Abrahams's thought in an unambiguously racist direction. South Africa apparently exacts a very heavy toll on some of its expatriated artists, a few of whom wind up infected with the very disease that caused them to quit that country. Abrahams's view from Coyaba, a place high in the Red Hills of Jamaica, was blinded by blatant xenophobia.

Abrahams's peculiar career enables us to trace in the life and work of one exiled South African author a pattern that reveals how changes in the relationship between a writer and his native land can bring about changes in his art, both for better and for worse. With another writer the pattern might be altogether different, though it seems likely that a brief visit to the homeland would generate a flurry of creative energy, as it did in Abrahams's case. For exile is not just a geographical dislocation; it is a state of mind as well, a state as balanced or unbalanced as personal circumstances permit. Some writers will go on reliving memories in book after book; others will move on to fresh imaginative terrain and seek fulfillment in new experiences and new commitments. But for most, the tug of the motherland, like that of an unsevered umbilical cord, will probably be sharp enough to produce strong emotions and a desire to cry out, if only to express pain or pleasure at being reminded so forcefully of the lingering hold of a vestigial attachment. For writers in exile, as for writers anywhere else, there may well be no place like home.

---

[1] For a fuller discussion of Abrahams's career up to this point, see Wade, Ogungbesan, and Ensor.

The Rise and Fall of Mbongeni Ngema

1996 has not been a good year for Mbongeni Ngema. Since early January he has been assailed in South African media not only by scores of journalists, television and radio commentators, news analysts and cartoonists, but also by numerous members of parliament, medical practitioners, fellow theatre directors, drama critics, outspoken ordinary citizens, and a government-appointed Public Protector. The fuss was largely over money, but it also had to do with art, government and disease—a volatile combination that kept the story on the front pages because it had real life and death implications. No one actually went so far as to call Ngema a murderer, but his manner of responding to the charges leveled against him, which ranged from rapacious greed and financial mismanagement to artistic incompetence and egomania, may have so alienated his national audience that he unwittingly may have put a premature end to his own spectacular career as a showman. He may have committed a form of professional suicide.

This is a pity, for he clearly is a talented actor, musician and director who through his own abundant energy and enterprise has made a major contribution to the development of black theatre in South Africa. His life, recounted sympathetically by Laura Jones in a biography entitled *Nothing Except Ourselves: The Harsh Times and Bold Theater of South Africa's Mbongeni Ngema*, is a classic rags-to-riches saga replete with the usual mixture of archetypal ingredients: hard work, perseverance, self-reliance, resourcefulness, skill, a pinch of good luck, and in the end, a pot of gold.

Success on the stage has been his hallmark. In the past fifteen years no other South African has won so many prestigious local and international awards in the performing arts—more than fifty in all, including the Edinburgh Festival's Fringe First Award, the Los Angeles Drama Critics Award, and an Obie Award Special Citation for *Woza Albert!*; a Tony nomination and several AA Mutual Life Vita Awards for *Asinamali!*; five Tony nominations and a Hollywood contract for *Sarafina!*; a Drama Desk Award nomination for *Township Fever!*; and a share of a Grammy Award for producing part of the sound track on Disney's *The Lion King*.[1] One would have thought that with a track record like this, Ngema was destined to succeed in whatever theatrical enterprise he undertook. What then went wrong? Why did his most recent venture into musical drama fail so abysmally? What ultimately brought him down?

A brief recap of his career may be helpful here. After serving a short period of apprenticeship with Gibson Kente, a popular township playwright and director, Ngema made his first big splash by teaming up with another of Kente's performers, Percy Mtwa, and creating a series of sketches built on the premise of Jesus Christ's second coming, this time to South Africa. Under the guidance of Barney Simon, an experienced theatre director, their two-man show, originally called *Our Father Who Art in Heaven*, opened at the Market Theatre in Johannesburg as *Woza Albert!* and immediately made an impact, drawing a larger black audience to that innovative theatre than any previous production (Jones 110). An extensive tour of the townships and black homelands followed, and the fame of *Woza Albert!* spread. It was an easy play to transport because the props consisted of little more than a couple of crates and a coat rack holding several items of clothing that the actors put on to impersonate various characters. To play white men, each actor clapped on a clown's nose—half a squash ball painted pink that was secured around his neck with an elastic band. This was minimalist theatre requiring no elaborate stage sets, fine costumes or fancy equipment. It could be done anywhere. The play relied entirely on the mimetic talents of the actors, who provided all the sound effects as well as an extraordinary range of visual effects.

After proving themselves locally, Ngema and Mtwa took their show to Britain, Germany and America, where it continued to be a smash hit, winning awards wherever it went. It remained abroad for nearly three years, and in the intervals between tours, Ngema returned to South Africa, founded his own small theatre company called Committed Artists, and trained a group of young men in performance techniques. He has said:

> In 1983 I established Committed Artists with the sole aim of training young, disadvantaged South Africans. My methodology entailed a combination of western and African theatrical techniques. Grotowsky, Stanislavsky and Peter Brook were the main western influences on my method, particularly with their experimental theatre (what Peter Brook called the immediate theatre). The African sphere was the most accented, especially the Zulu culture. This is what made this method unique, for African life and movement has a rhythm of its own. (Ngema vii)

In 1985 Committed Artists launched their first production, *Asinamali!* (We have no money!), in a cinema in Soweto, then moved it downtown to the Market Theatre before embarking on very successful national and international tours. *Asinamali!* had the same kind of intense energy that distinguished *Woza Albert!*, but it made much greater use of song, dance and tightly organized ensemble work. It also dealt in an unusual manner with the tragic lives of five men imprisoned after the assassination of a prominent strike leader. Peter Brook saw the production in Harlem and was struck by its dynamism, noting that

> If you approach a situation like the South African one naturalistically, you can't present terrible events like these in any other than a tragic, sentimental way. The events in their very nature are tragic or sentimentality-producing events. But what I found profoundly right and extraordinary about *Asinamali!* was that this

180 • African Textualities

> horrifying situation was being presented, pitilessly, through a *joie de vivre*. The events were not softened by it, but heightened to the last degree because they were presented, not through a sentimentality, but through a vitality. (Jones 114-15)

Ngema was not one of the performers in this play, but he had trained all the actors, written the script, composed the songs, and choreographed the dances. *Asinamali!* was his first great success as a director-producer, and he often traveled with the company when they performed in America, Europe, Japan and Australia, a tour that lasted more than two years.

Whenever he returned to South Africa, he went out and searched for fresh talent, simultaneously recruiting experienced theatre professionals to help him with his next show, which he decided would celebrate South Africa's black schoolchildren who were then leading the struggle against apartheid. He rounded up twenty teenagers, "moved them into a four-room house in Daveytown, near Johannesburg, lived with them, and trained them vocally, mentally and physically" (Jones 124). At the same time he developed a script, composing songs and writing lyrics as he went along. After fourteen months of hard work and fine tuning, the result was *Sarafina!*, his most ambitious undertaking and by far his most remunerative. After opening to great applause at the Market Theatre, Ngema in 1987 took his cast of twenty-three youngsters to Lincoln Center in New York where their engagement was extended repeatedly until they moved to Broadway and played to capacity audiences at the Cort Theatre for the next eighteen months (Jones 129). "*Sarafina!* was probably the highlight of my career," Ngema has said, adding, "Ironically, it was the least sophisticated of all my work" (Lee 34). The story-line, he admitted, "is not strong. It's very simplistic...[But] I did it deliberately. I was telling it through the eyes of the kids. And those kids, wearing those uniforms...people just loved them. It's easier to love young people than adults on stage...For the first time in South Africa, we saw a young professional cast. We saw a Broadway musical played by kids, who, even though they were young, were highly professional. You, see, it's not so much the story but how it's done!" (Berman 32).

It could be said that at that point in his career, Ngema seemed to be doing everything right. He was offered recording contracts, an Academy-Award winning director made a full-length documentary about *Sarafina!*, and then came the Hollywood version of the musical with megastar Whoopi Goldberg in a leading role. This feature film, shot in the environs of Soweto, employed about 100 actors and up to 5000 extras (Makgabutlane 1992: 40). By the time it hit the big screen in 1992, *Sarafina!* had been running continuously on the stage for five years.

And during this period, Ngema had not been idle. Thriving on his success, he tirelessly "assembled a second company, rehearsed them in Johannesburg, and sent them on a tour of Europe and Japan. In 1989, this company went to Paris and performed at Peter Brook's Bouffes du Nord as part of a nationwide celebration of the bicentennial of the French Revolution" (Jones 131). There were also *Sarafina!* revivals in London and New York. As apartheid crumbled, audiences abroad simply couldn't get enough of this show.

Throughout these years, the money just kept rolling in, and Ngema's ambitions grew accordingly. By 1990 he had a new show, *Township Fever!*, ready for production. Bigger than anything he had done before, this involved thirty-six actors plus a thirteen-piece band and dealt with the murder of four scab workers during a 1987 railway strike in South Africa. Ngema has said,

> I was fascinated by the idea that people without any criminal record could be compelled to commit gruesome acts totally out of character with their personalities and their morality under the forces of...a "pressure cooker situation"...The desperation of these workers got to me...*Township Fever* is about music, about Johannesburg, about Soweto, about Mshengu Village, about the homelands and about how our environment plays upon us. Apartheid dehumanises the oppressed—but it also dehumanises the oppressors. (Ngema 128-29)

To get this message across, Ngema relied on his usual bag of tricks: lively mbaqanga music, energetic dancing, athletic performances, a mixture of sentiment and *joie de vivre*—the kind of theatrical experience Peter Brook recognized as possessing "vitality." In an interview Ngema explained his "philosophy of theatre" this way:

> I think it is because I am a musician that I tend to have the kind of approach I have. When theatre does not have a beat, does not have a rhythm, then theatre tends to bore. Theatre must be like a piece of music which has a beat that people can sit and listen to...or dance to. And within that beat there are so many other colours you put in. But first and foremost, theatre should entertain. When people are entertained, then they will be informed and enlightened. The vehicle we use is entertainment, first of all. (Makgabutlane 1990: 20)

However, at this point in his career, given his past successes, the audience he appears to have sought most avidly to entertain was an international one, and this may have led him to blunt the political force of his message. In interviews published a few weeks after *Township Fever!* opened, he stated,

> You see, when people pay $70 for a ticket, they do not want to hear about the sufferings of black people from a strange country in Africa. They want to be entertained. (Mendel 18)
> They are not gonna be bored by you telling them about your struggle in South Africa. They don't care about South Africa. Those people want to go and see a good theatre piece. Finished. Whether it's a South African piece, a Jamaican piece, a British piece, they just want to see good theatre. In fact, they are a harder audience to entertain. Most of the time they do not see political theatre anyway; they refuse to go to fringe theatre in New York City. They do not go off-Broadway or off-off Broadway because they don't want to hear politics. Those are the ladies with fur coats. (Makgabutlane 1990: 24)

By now Ngema may have been aiming his productions at New York ladies in fur coats rather than at his own people. Certainly he had his eye on the main chance—a production that would culminate in a screen adaptation, just as *Sarafina!* had. In a 1992 interview he said, "The story told in *Township Fever* (which followed in the footsteps of *Sarafina!*) is a more powerful story. I am at the moment talking with studios in Hollywood. If someone came to me and said, 'Here's R10-million, let's make a movie,' I would go for it" (Makgabutlane 1992: 40).

Money, in fact, had become a major preoccupation for him at the very height of his success, when he was simultaneously touring two *Sarafina!* companies, negotiating film rights for the Whoopi Goldberg production, and training the large troupe of actors in *Township Fever!* "My company is funding itself on huge budgets," he exclaimed. "Before we staged *Township Fever*, we were talking half a million!" (Mendel 19)

He had other projects up his sleeve, too. Asked in 1990 what his plans were, he said, "I wish I had more money. I want to start my own record company. In fact, I am in the process of doing it. It might take a year or two. And then maybe later go into movies" (Makgabutlane 1990: 24). Five years afterwards, asked "what single thing would improve the quality of your life?" his answer was unequivocal: "Money, money, money" (Metsoamere 8).

Not that he hadn't already made a small fortune. In fact, by 1994 he had earned enough to buy himself a nice house with a kidney-shaped swimming pool and a sunken tennis court in an affluent white community in Bryanston, a suburb north of Johannesburg (Jones 144-46). A year later he had also fulfilled his dream of starting a record company, Mbongeni Ngema Productions, which has by now produced at least four albums and CDs (Anon., *Tribute* 10), and he had launched a film company as well, Mbongeni Ngema Films, which currently has two films in the pipeline, one of them based on the life of Winnie Mandela (Isaacson 2). In addition he recently published a collection of his musical librettos called *The Best of Mbongeni Ngema*, and since January 1994 he has been serving as a salaried director of musical theatre at Durban's Natal Playhouse, where three of his own new musicals have been produced. All in all, one could say that life has not been unkind to Mbongeni Ngema. And to give him his due, one would have to concede that he certainly has taken full advantage of the opportunities available to him, capitalizing on them whenever he could. He has worked very hard and he has prospered.

But ever since the original *Sarafina!* caught the world's attention and made him a wealthy man, his career has been on a downward trajectory. The trouble started with *Township Fever!*, which offended the leadership of COSATU, the labor union federation that had ordered the execution of the scabs killed during the 1987 railway strike. Ngema was accused by union officials of co-opting, "for his own commercial gain, a major event in the people's struggle" and of personalizing a communal tragedy by adapting it to his own life as a musician (Jones 148-49). Drama critics also didn't like the show, feeling Ngema had "devoted too much energy to the music and not enough to the script, which badly needed editing. A few critics suggested that he should have delegated some of the work to collaborators" (Jones 151). He was simply trying to take on too much and, as a consequence, was losing creative control of his own gigantic production. It wasn't a matter of him being too big for his britches; the problem was the reverse: his britches were too big for him.

His next show, *Magic at 4 a.m.*, was another musical extravaganza, this one originally inspired by Muhammad Ali's 1974 fight against George Foreman in Zaire. In fact, it was at first "envisioned simplistically as a South African tribute to the champ" (Jones 163), a kind of black *Rocky*, the sort of show that would have tremendous box-office appeal and motion picture potential. Ngema invited his biographer Laura Jones to collaborate on the libretto, and her concluding chapter in *Nothing Except Ourselves*, describing the shaping of the production, is the fullest account available in print of Ngema's characteristic *modus operandi*.

He usually starts with a vague concept—in this case one prompted by a meeting with Ali and his handlers, who attended the New York première of the Hollywood film of *Sarafina!* He then seeks backing for the development of the script (provided at the outset by a theatre in New Jersey), negotiates a suitable venue for the performance (this time the mammoth, 1,100-seat Civic Theatre instead of the smaller Market Theatre), assembles a large company ("well over fifty, not including lovers, families, and other hangers-on," Jones 166), and starts putting them through drills ("doing calisthenics, singing scales, and learning dances," Jones 168) before actually tackling the task of writing the book, music and lyrics his Committed Artists would perform.

But once he has a deadline for his show, he goes at it full-throttle. Jones reports that he and she brainstormed a structure for the play by sitting up nights in a friend's shebeen:

We knew that our hero would be a worker and amateur boxer living in a war-torn, single-sex hostel. His very life would be a homage to Muhammad Ali, his idol, whose example would keep him from willingly partaking in wars he doesn't believe in...We chose against setting our hostel in Soweto or any other major township and decided to place it in a workers' compound at a fictitious gold mine on the outskirts...The story elements were a little disjointed and confusing at this point, but we had fun sorting them out and pulling them together during our first month of work together...As usual in Mbongeni's work, the basis for this play was the company. The "magic at 4 a.m.," the Ali-Foreman fight that had been Mbongeni's starting point, moved to a subordinate position in our imagery. The story changed every time Mbongeni promoted a bit player to a supporting role. Very early on, he had chosen his brother Bhoyi to play the lead. Bhoyi, who had been training in a boxing gym for weeks before I arrived in Johannesburg, came to me frequently during that first month begging for hints about his character, concerned that the job would be too big for him. But Bhoyi needn't have worried; his part was built to fit him, to be filled by him, as all the roles were designed to illuminate unique characteristics of the actors who played them. (The music worked much the same way. Mbongeni hired all his favorite musicians—including his old friend Skhumbuzo, the guitarist—and as he wrote songs was often inspired by what he knew they could do with them.) The remaining members of the cast would be featured as dancers or singers, according to their strengths. (Jones 169-72)

After two months of this kind of resourceful improvisation, with Mbongeni writing music by day and collaborating on the script by night, Jones wrote to a friend that "Since December 20 an entire story has been dreamed up, a script written, a set designed, more than 25 songs composed and, now, orchestrated (an 11-piece band has joined us in the rehearsal room), and a few of the numbers have been choreographed, although Mbongeni is saving that job for last" (Jones 180).

This left two months for final rehearsals, which characteristically ran up to sixteen hours straight, usually into the wee hours of the morning. On opening night, Jones records,

the play ran an epic three and a half hours, a good deal shorter than it had been in the rehearsal room, but still too long: a fault underlined in every review I read—most positive, some mixed, a few spiteful. In the following weeks, we continued to work on the play, and we cut a half hour out of it—most of it from the musical finale—before the scheduled closing night in July. (Before the play begins to tour outside South Africa, it will certainly change again.) (Jones 187)

This was written in 1993, and until now *Magic at 4 a.m.* has never been performed outside South Africa and has never been made into a feature film. *Township Fever!* had a brief run in New York, but it too never got picked up by Hollywood. Another recent show, *Mama!*, based on *A Chorus Line* and staged with middling success at Ngema's Natal Playhouse in 1995, has not yet gone overseas. Perhaps the ladies in fur coats would not be sufficiently entertained by these topical mega-musicals. Perhaps after the first *Sarafina!* Ngema gradually lost his golden touch.

The failure in South Africa of his latest musical, which was a sequel to *Sarafina!*, may be attributed in part to Ngema's improvisational working methods and in part to his concept of himself at the equivalent of a Broadway or Hollywood producer. But *Sarafina 2* really flopped because it grew far too large, its expansion being encouraged and augmented by procedural errors made by officials in the government's Department of Health who approved a gargantuan budget of 14,247,600 rands (ca. £2.5 million or nearly $4 million then) for the musical out of funds donated by the European Union to combat the spread of AIDS in South Africa (Coan 9). Indeed, most of the attacks on the production have been directed not at Ngema himself but at Health Minister Dr. Nkosazana Zuma whose oversight of the tendering procedure that won Ngema such a lucrative contract appears to have been characterized by another type of oversight—i.e., by negligence.

No one denies that her intentions were good. Her idea was to use theatre as a means of educating young South Africans, especially those in the townships and rural areas, about the serious dangers posed today by casual, unprotected sexual intercourse—specifically the mortal danger of contracting AIDS. What better way to do this than to employ South Africa's most successful and most popular black director to mount a musical on this theme, a show that could travel on a year-long bus and truck tour to township halls, cinemas, shopping centers, schools and rural communities in all corners of the country? On her own initiative she approached Ngema about this in June 1995, suggesting that the production be launched on December 1st, World AIDS Day (Davis 4).

Ngema was keen on the idea and "gave an off-the-cuff estimate of R800,000; Zuma subsequently set the ceiling at R5 million, but Health Department officials ultimately signed a R14,2 million contract with Ngema" (Carter 4). Worse yet, these officials skirted regulations governing standard bidding procedures on state contracts. There may have been some urgency about getting the show on the road, but their carelessness in following established guidelines was to cost Dr. Zuma many subsequent headaches. When the story hit the press, there were calls for her dismissal or immediate resignation, and the ANC-led government was faulted for its lack of transparency in accounting for expenditures made from funds donated by the European Union to improve public health in South Africa. *Sarafina 2* rapidly became a scandal.

Ngema himself had ambitious plans for this sequel to his most famous show. A month before it opened he said,

> We will touch the people in every corner, and all colours of the nation...We are speaking to all of South Africa this time. Although *Sarafina!* (1) played on Broadway, and in Europe and Britain, the majority of South Africans didn't see the first *Sarafina!* It ran in Durban for three weeks—after playing five years in the rest of the world! This time we are aiming to reach 10 percent of the South African population. Perhaps in a few years time we will take the show to Broadway, but at this point in my life, my Broadway is my people. We need to perform to them...Many people have been craving to see the live production of *Sarafina!*, but I was not comfortable to bring back theatre that related to fighting for freedom—when we are actually free! So the idea of a sequel was born...it is no longer the fight for freedom, it is the fight for human survival. (Anon., *Citizen* 23)

Big words, big ambitions, big show, extremely big budget. Ngema had set about assembling a company of between seventy and eighty singers, dancers, musicians, and crew, many of them veterans from his previous shows, some of them his relatives and friends. To play the lead role he selected the original Sarafina, Leleti Khumalo, who by then was his second wife. According to early reports, "The updated story sees Sarafina now a social worker but still very much in touch with school children who look upon her as a role model. She gives inspiration to students who are trying to get a concert together at a school in rural Zululand" (Anon., *D'Arts* 21). Does this recycled plot sound familiar? To provide further continuity, Ngema repeated several songs from the first *Sarafina!* even though these had nothing to do with the theme of the new show (Makoe 3).

But there was new material too, some of it very explicitly concerned with AIDS. Part of the story-line focuses on "a popular high school girl who contracts the disease, sparking off an intense debate between pupils, the teacher, the nurse, the social worker and traditional healers on how to deal with this situation" (V. Ngema 7). Some reviewers felt that the play was too didactic and said too much too stridently about AIDS; others felt that it did not provide enough basic information about the transmission of the disease; still others claimed that a good deal of the information offered was inaccurate and potentially dangerous to teenagers. Ngema was accused of confusing "the use of words like AIDS, HIV and *Ngculazi*. He uses all these words as though they mean the same thing. According to the play, the only way a person can get AIDS is by sleeping with many partners, which in real life is not true" (Khumalo 7). There were complaints that some of the messages about AIDS, besides being "confusing and ineffective...were definitely degrading to women" (Robbins 1). One disappointed viewer who was HIV-positive walked out of the show in anger and disappointment, saying he could not cope with "such a blatant downplaying of this serious disease...They've taken a topic of genocidal proportions for a musical, thus making a joke of it. It's equivalent to making a musical of the Holocaust...By interval the only thing I [had] learned about AIDS was that once diagnosed as positive, you have to go to church and trust in God" (Anon., *Cape Times* 1).

Ngema clearly had not properly researched the problem *Sarafina 2* was exploring and exploiting. He was operating from a set of vague concepts—that promiscuity leads to AIDS, that young people are especially at risk, that condoms are the answer to the problem—but he seems to have been less concerned with articulating a responsible social message than he was with expressing a rhythmic song-and-dance medium. He once said,

First and foremost, I'm an entertainer. And when I have entertained you, then I want to inform you, in that way I move you...My theatre must enlighten. The audiences must walk out of the theatre having learnt something...I direct as a musician. I see my theatre pieces as one song, as a whole, as a piece of jazz which changes beat, changes colours...What excites me is when the script and music become one, when a performance comes together...People must walk out and say "WOW!" (Mendel 19)

In the case of *Sarafina 2*, people were walking out unenlightened and saying "WOW!" for all the wrong reasons.

Some, including a few who were most critical of the show, applauded its "dazzling brilliance" and "flawless" music and choreography (V. Ngema 7), its "precision lighting, dance routines and beautiful faces" (Spratt 1), its "grand scale...ineluctable magnetism...disciplined energy [and] magnificent assault on the senses" (MacLiam 1), its "glitz and glamour" (MacLiam 7). But despite such virtues, the general consensus among spectators was that *Sarafina 2* was "a loose, uncontrolled musical desperately looking for a story to tell" (V. Ngema 7), that there was "no drama in the entire play" (Khumalo 7), that "it was the same old vague outline of nubile, nay, fat slags, with breasts and a great love for shaking their bottoms about" who moved awkwardly from "swing-your-pants stuff to straight lecturing to the audience" (Ramklown 5), and that the show was far too long and needed trimming "by as much as half an hour" (MacLiam 1). Obviously *Sarafina 2* had failed not only to enlighten but also to entertain.

What drew most criticism, however, was the show's stupendous cost. As more and more budgetary details leaked out in the press, public fury grew. Taxpayers were shocked to learn

—that Ngema was receiving a salary of R300,000 for the production, this on top of his normal salary of R90,000 as Musical Director of the Natal Playhouse;

—that R1.1 million had been spent on a luxury bus for the cast, a bus equipped with a private toilet;

—that monthly salaries for administrative staff included R10,000 for an administrator, R8,000 for a company manager, R6,000 for an assistant director, R5,000 for a senior secretary, and R4,000 each for two additional secretaries—salaries considered excessive for such work;

—that the five principal members of the cast received R2,000 each per week, and the eight sub-principals R1,200 each per week, whereas professional AIDS workers in South Africa were paid only R2,000 per month;

—that fourteen musicians received R1,500 each per week, members of the chorus R700 each per week, and two bus drivers and two truck drivers R2,000 each per month;

—that everyone involved in the production also received a subsistence allowance of R50 per day for 365 days;

—that other budget categories seemed unusually inflated: R32,000 for two cellular phones, R50,000 for programmes; R50,000 for scenery, R100,000 for costumes, R200,000 for security equipment, R300,000 for four security guards, R1.2 million for lighting and sound equipment, R1.4 million for office rentals and equipment. (Stuart 1; Nyatsumba 18; Anon., *City Press* 2)

Worse still, it came out that in the first three months that *Sarafina 2* was on stage, R1.1 million had disappeared in unauthorized expenditures, that bookkeeping was not up to scratch, and that there was no control over petty cash (Davis 5). Money simply vanished without a trace.

On top of all this, Ngema was being allowed to charge R20 for admission to this government-sponsored show, a fee much too high for most of its intended audience. In its first hundred days in Kwazulu-Natal, only 5,868 people had seen the 36 performances of *Sarafina 2*, an average of 163 per night (Ngidi 4). The numbers picked up dramatically in March when the show moved to Soweto's Eyethu Cinema and the admission fee for schoolchildren was dropped; 1300 people flocked to the opening night (Chisholm 1), but within a few weeks only 80 spectators were turning up for a Saturday afternoon performance (Gevisser 14). It was by now clear that this expensive vehicle would never succeed in reaching a tenth of the South African population.

However, the show might have gone on to the end of the year had Ngema kept his mouth shut. Stung by the negative press he was receiving, he responded by thumping his chest and talking back. He claimed that

> When the minister had this idea [of spreading information about AIDS through a theatrical production], it was clear in her mind she wanted me to do the play. There is no one else with an international track record and there was no one else who could produce this kind of play and draw in crowds of black people to the theatre. (van der Walt and Sole 1)

In a later interview he boldly asserted "I am the best artist in the country. That's the reason why they contracted me" (Scott 16). The play had received bad reviews, he said, "because 'my people' cannot appreciate a 'Broadway class' production" (Anon., *Daily Dispatch* 14). Furthermore, the attitude of South African journalists had been "Let's find another famous black man and shoot him down" (Scott 16).

He expanded on these views in a lengthy interview with Mark Gevisser of the *Mail and Guardian*, recorded as follows:

> About the bus he says, "Yes! It's about time our artists were transported in dignity. Why must we be transported in luxury buses in the United States, but come to our own country to be put in the back of Kombis? No way! I'm proud of our bus."
>
> Are his own services worth R300,000, particularly given the fact that he is paid another full-time salary, worth R90,000, by the state through his position as musical director of the Natal Playhouse? "No, they are not. I should be earning at least a million." But does any director in this country earn those figures? "I don't think you can compare me to anyone in this country."
>
> He is unrepentant about the cost of the production, putting a race-spin on it: "I'm not prepared to do a second-class production. Why should whites get state-funded first-class productions in the State Theatre, while blacks in the townships get flatbed trucks? No. Blacks deserve Broadway standards...

What I'm doing with Sarafina II is an exact continuation of what I was doing with the original Sarafina. The only difference is that when we were doing freedom theatre, the government wouldn't pay for it. Now we are free, we are shifting to other stories, and the government is finally paying." (16)

The public reaction to these remarks was swift and censorious. Ngema was condemned for his "stupendous arrogance" (Nyatsumba 18), for knowing "next to nothing about the discipline of educating through drama" (Mondear 16), for having "woven a slight and trivial message through a production which he was going to mount anyway, in order to secure funding which should have been deployed elsewhere" (Mondear 16). One journalist wanted to know

How much...has Ngema paid his actors in his other plays? Seeing that he has been immensely successful as a playwright, why is it that he has not previously used his not inconsiderable resources to buy his cast the R1-million luxury bus so that it could indeed travel "in dignity"? Could it be that it was only when the R14,27-million was made available to him to produce an AIDS play that he suddenly realized that the "dignity" of his cast was important? (Nyatsumba 18)

Another journalist pointed out that

Apart from the fact that [Ngema] is now a senior official at one of these "white" state institutions [he criticizes], where he has successfully produced three of his own plays using state money, the problem here is that he—as a creative artist—is dealing with the Health Department's budget as if it were funding for the arts rather than funding for health education...He was frequently slammed, in the 1980s, for capitalizing on the struggle. Is he now capitalizing on another? (Gevisser 16)

Even fellow playwrights began to speak out against Ngema's squandering of state resources. Gibson Kente, Ngema's mentor, said, "The play carries an important message. It is beautifully presented but I think the money is a bit too much...For that money, you can produce about 90 dramatic episodes [in a television series]. That could draw many more viewers and the message would reach many people...I think the play should have been dramatised (instead of being a musical)" (Mashego 15). Matsemela Manaka agreed about the extravagant budget, maintaining, "It is shocking that so much money could be given to an individual when there is such a big need to fund the arts" (Mashego 15). Jerry Skosana suggested, "We have institutions rendering (AIDS education) services. The money should have gone to them. And some of the money should, at least, have gone to schools, where sex education must be implemented" (Mashego 15). Another KwaZulu-Natal playwright, who asked to remain anonymous, put forward the view that "the money should have been given to directors in all nine provinces. In that way, the message would reach people quicker" (Mashego 15).

It was also pointed out that other theatre groups in the country had been carrying out very effective AIDS education work for some time with little or no official sponsorship; among these were the Tivoneleni Vavasati AIDS Awareness Project, a women's theatre group operating since 1991 in rural areas of the Northern Province (Tivoneleni); the African Research and Education Puppetry Programme (Arepp) which had been running for nine years a popular "Puppets Against AIDS" play that was now reaching about 200,000 people each year in a countrywide network of clinics, schools, community centers, AIDS groups and civic associations (Simon 1); and Aidslink, another non-governmental organization that had developed an educational drama on AIDS to tour Gauteng informal settlements for four months (Simon 2). All these organizations were doing their work on very small budgets and without access to luxury buses, expensive lighting and sound equipment, or lavish salaries. Asked if he had seen *Sarafina 2*, Gary Friedman, creator of Puppets Against AIDS, replied, "I can't afford it at R20" (Coan 9).

Faced with a relentless daily barrage of criticism in the press, the ANC-led government had to do something about *Sarafina 2*. At first they stood loyally behind Minister Zuma, leaving the matter to be investigated impartially by a newly appointed National Public Protector, Selby Baqwa. But the Department of Health also sought to control the damage by calling Ngema on the carpet and asking him to make substantial changes in the play. When it was learned in May that one option they were considering was issuing a videotape of the musical so that more people could see it, a video that might cost the government at least another R2 million, of which Ngema was to receive an undisclosed sum, the clamor grew louder, with most opponents insisting that this would be throwing more good money after bad (Lund 1-2; Anon., *Eastern Province Herald* 4). A month later, after the Public Protector published his report documenting serious administrative bungling in the *Sarafina 2* affair, the Department of Health finally pulled the plug on the play, Dr. Zuma announcing it would no longer be funded by her Department but "by the private sector, although she did not give details" (Cull 2). The cancellation of the contract would save the government about R5 million of the R14,27 million allocation.

This resolution of the matter did not satisfy all commentators. A columnist for the *Natal Witness* remarked that

> one of the most shameful aspects of the *Sarafina* saga is that Mbongeni Ngema will remain not only unscathed but richer for his involvement with "AIDS education." A disciple of KZN Premier Frank Mdlalose's dictum that "extravagance is a relative term," Ngema's response to the controversy has been to welcome the publicity it brought to the play. Relieved of the obligation actually to promote AIDS education, the government's withdrawal from the project "is just perfect for me." Now he can go ahead and con audiences with a piece of work that months after its launch was still so shoddy that he would not let the press review it. As for the money: "Maybe R14 million is a lot of money to us South Africans but it is not to everyone in the world."

More important to Ngema than AIDS education, wasted money, unprofessional work, fraudulent tenders and government accountability, is what it has all done for Ngema. "My only competition for the front pages was Nelson Mandela...I have seen Ngema on the front page and Mandela on the inside pages some days." So much for humility. Maybe he'll be offered a post as minister of maladministration. For the moment, however, he's looking forward to *Sarafina* making so much money that R14 million will seem more insignificant to him than it already appears now. "If you have the numbers you have the power," he says of the audiences he hopes will attend his show. He could have taken the words right out of the government's mouth. Ruling by numbers means never having to say Sorryfina. (Vanderhaeghen 6)

One gets the impression from Ngema's bemused and insensitive remarks that he is still supremely self-confident about his abilities and unapologetic about his behavior, that in fact he is treating the whole *Sarafina 2* fiasco as a huge joke and laughing his way to the bank. But it is difficult to believe that he will "remain not only unscathed but richer for his involvement with 'AIDS education.'" Granted, he may have made a considerable amount of money in the past year, but no one is likely to forget in the years to come how he made it: by trying to bring a bit of Broadway—bloated budgets, tinsel and all—to the back streets and backwaters of South Africa; by singing and dancing his way through a medical pandemic without being fully aware that he was toying (or toyi-toying) with people's lives; by blithely and brazenly profiteering from his own people's present and future misery.

AIDS is already a devastating phenomenon in South Africa. No one knows how many South Africans have been infected with the HIV virus, but conservative estimates range as high as 7 million, or one-seventh of a total population of 49 million (du Bois 10). In March 1995 the *Daily News* reported that an average of 20.13% of pregnant women at Durban's King Edward VIII hospital tested HIV positive. By July 1996 the rate had gone up to 25% (Anon., *Natal Witness* 4). At the Pietermaritzburg Boom Street Clinic the HIV infection rate for men and women treated for sexually transmitted diseases is even higher, ranging between 54 and 62% in April, May and June of 1996 (Anon., *Natal Witness* 4). All these statistics come from KwaZulu-Natal, the province thought to have the highest incidence of HIV in South Africa. This is Ngema's home territory, so it is more than a little disconcerting to learn that his funding for *Sarafina 2* was double the KwaZulu-Natal AIDS budget for the year ending March 1996 (Sherriffs 15).

The World Bank estimates that "by the year 2005, 600,000 South Africans will have contracted [full-blown] AIDS, and between 300 and 500 people would be dying daily from the disease" (Stuart 2). However, the European Union, which had contributed R100 million to the South African Health Department, "just under half of it specifically earmarked for AIDS programmes" (Anon., *Saturday Paper* 1), was recently reported to be considering withdrawing its funding in the wake of the *Sarafina 2* scandal (Sidley 4). Ngema's legacy to his countrymen could thus translate very quickly into an accelerated AIDS death rate in the next decade. And it may be this morbid fact that South Africans will remember best about *Sarafina 2*—not the dancing, not the singing, not all the glitz and glamour, but the flagrantly wasted opportunity to save and protect human life through effective theatrical intervention in a national health crisis. Mbongeni Ngema, the carefree, cavalier, Broadway-spoiled villain in this drama, by then may have been hissed off the South African stage.

---

[1] Ngema ultimately was declared ineligible for this award due to a technicality (Coleman).

Ken Saro-Wiwa: In Short, a Giant

The Fonlon-Nichols Award[1] is meant to honor two singular achievements: excellence in creative writing and contributions to the struggle for human rights. To those who draw a sharp distinction between art and politics, this might seem a dubious conjunction of disparate accomplishments. Indeed, some might charge the creators of this award with attempting an impossible alchemical feat—the meltdown and fusion in a single medal of the unalloyed properties of two Nobel Prizes, one for Literature, the other for Peace.

Yet the African Literature Association, since its inception, has always acclaimed a connection between creativity and commitment, between writing good works and doing good deeds. It is therefore altogether fitting that the ALA should seek to pay tribute to talented authors who display a deep engagement both with the page and with their age. Such authors are to be commended for taking their wider social responsibilities seriously. They write not only for self-expression but also for group expression, putting their words to the service of a community, and by so doing, giving an articulate voice to the unheard, the unheeded, the voiceless. Instead of just sitting and writing, they are known as well for standing and fighting. They display a higher morality which is based on a profound double allegiance: a loyalty to literature and a respect for life. It is this combination of commitments that the Fonlon-Nichols Award is intended to recognize and reward.

This year the award goes to Ken Saro-Wiwa, one of Nigeria's most prolific and popular writers. For some time now Saro-Wiwa has been spearheading a move to safeguard the rights of the Ogoni, a small ethnic group in an oil-rich area of South-central Nigeria that has been impoverished by exploitation of its lands by the Nigerian Government and various Western oil companies. Ogoni rivers have become polluted, destroying the livelihood of fishermen, and natural gas burnoffs have polluted the air, endangering the health of everyone in the region. When the Ogoni attempted to protest their plight a few years ago, federal troops marched in, burnt hundreds of homes, and killed scores of protesters. In response, Saro-Wiwa formed a Movement for the Survival of the Ogoni People (MOSOP), drafted an Ogoni Bill of Rights, wrote numerous articles for Nigerian media on maltreatment of his people, and tried to bring the situation to the attention of the United Nations. He also made a documentary film detailing the suffering and repression of the Ogoni. For these efforts he was imprisoned for treason by the Babangida Government in June of 1993; he was released by a new Nigerian Government a few months later, but it was feared that he might still face trial or other political repercussions for his outspoken activism.

Such threats have not silenced him. In January this year he testified before a commission of inquiry investigating recent ethnic clashes in which over 400 Ogoni were killed. He continues to speak up fearlessly for his people and for others who have been denied basic human rights in Nigeria. In his Presidential Address at the 1992 conference of the Association of Nigerian Authors he said

> Human rights is the only guarantee of peaceful co-existence of peoples, the insurance of justice for individuals and groups. Denied, it creates conditions of social and political unrest and often leads to violence and conflict...I therefore consider it a worthy service to humanity and a patriotic duty to protest the denial of rights to individuals and communities. (16)

Saro-Wiwa has lived by this creed.

But he has not been a full-time political activist. He has also distinguished himself as a Commissioner of the Rivers State, a successful businessman, a television producer, a newspaper columnist, a publisher, and an author of more than two dozen books. He may be best known in Nigeria for his popular television comedy series, *Basi and Company*, which ran for six years (1985-90), and is estimated to have attracted a viewing audience of more than thirty million every Wednesday night. In addition to producing this show, he recruited and trained its actors and actresses, and penned its more than 150 episodes himself. To keep even busier, he wrote widely for the press too, eventually starting his own column, "Similia," in the Lagos *Sunday Times*, which he filled with salty commentary on current Nigerian political, economic and cultural events. During this same hyperactive period his star was rising in the literary world, largely due to the success of his first novel, *Sozaboy* (1985), which had been written in an amusing experimental idiom he called "rotten English." And in his spare time he published volume after volume of his own poetry, short stories, plays, essays, folktales, children's literature, analyses of the Nigerian civil war, and narrative and dramatic spin-offs of his *Basi and Company* scripts. On one day in 1991, his fiftieth birthday, his own publishing house, Saros International Publishers, launched eight new titles by him. In this manner he has managed in less than a decade to establish himself as a veritable literary dynamo.

Despite the popular nature of much of his writing, Saro-Wiwa has won the respect of literary critics and commentators who appreciate his colloquial directness and vibrant humor but also commend his craft and underlying seriousness of purpose. Abiola Irele has called him "a major new figure in our national literature," an opinion borne out by the fact that more has been written about him in recent years than about any other Nigerian writers except such canonical colossi as Wole Soyinka and Chinua Achebe. Some of the press reports on Saro-Wiwa jokingly refer to him as a "short giant" or a vertically challenged giant, but it is clear that he is already looming high enough to cast a long shadow and that his energy and vitality have raised him far above many of his peers.

In his writing, in his politics, in his impulses, Saro-Wiwa is truly a man of the people. But unlike Chief Nanga, he is also, first and foremost, a man for the people. He writes to move people—to make them laugh, think, protest, act. And in his political work he moves to help people, defending them from injustice by pleading their case in the most conspicuous public arenas. In word and deed he has excelled as a champion of the little man and as an advocate of human rights for all people, regardless of size and stature. His achievements, his actions and his convictions make him a very worthy recipient of the 1994 Fonlon-Nichols Award.

[1] This citation was read when Ken Saro-Wiwa was presented with the Fonlon-Nichols Award at the 1994 African Literature Association conference in Accra.

Works Cited

Aarne, Antti, and Stith Thompson. *The Types of the Folktale: A Classification and Bibliography*. Helsinki: Suomalainen Tiedeakatemia, 1964.

Abrahams, Peter. *Dark Testament*. London: Allen & Unwin, 1942.

_____. *Song of the City*. London: Crisp, 1945.

_____. *Mine Boy*. London: Crisp, 1946.

_____. *The Path of Thunder*. New York: Harper, 1948.

_____. *Wild Conquest*. New York: Harper, 1950.

_____. *Return to Goli*. London: Faber & Faber, 1953.

_____. *Tell Freedom*. London: Faber & Faber, 1954.

_____. *A Wreath for Udomo*. London: Faber & Faber, 1956.

_____. *Jamaica: An Island Mosaic*. London: Her Majesty's Stationery Office/Corona, 1957.

_____. *A Night of Their Own*. London: Faber & Faber, 1965.

_____. *This Island Now*. London: Faber & Faber, 1985.

_____. *The View from Coyaba*. London and Boston: Faber & Faber, 1985.

Achebe, Chinua. *Things Fall Apart*. London: Heinemann, 1958.

_____. *No Longer at Ease*. London: Heinemann, 1960.

_____. *Arrow of God*. London: Heinemann, 1964.

_____. "The Role of the Writer in a New Nation." *Nigeria Magazine* 81 (1964): 157-60.

_____. "English and the African Writer." *Transition* 18 (1965): 27-30.

_____. "The Black Writer's Burden." *Présence Africaine* 59 (1966): 135-40.

_____. *A Man of the People*. London: Heinemann, 1966.

_____. "What Do African Intellectuals Read?" *Times Literary Supplement* 12 May 1972: 547.

_____. *Anthills of the Savannah*. London: Heinemann, 1987.

Adotevi, Stanislas. "Negritude is Dead: The Burial." *Journal of the New African Literature and the Arts* 7-8 (1969-70): 70-81.

Aeschylus. *The Agamemnon*. Trans. Gilbert Murray. London: Allen and Unwin, 1932.

Alvarez-Péreyre, Neela. "The Multicultural Encounter: On Asian South African Writers." *South African Literature: From Popular Culture to the Written Artefact*. Ed. Wolfgang Schäfer and Robert Kriger. Bad Boll, Germany: Evangelische Academy, 1988. 53-60.

Anon. "Bus-truck Tour for *Sarafina 2*." *Citizen* 3 November 1995: 23.

_____. "*Sarafina 2*." *D'Arts* December 1995-January 1996: 21.

_____. "Mbongeni Ngema, Director of Musical Theatre, NAPAC." *Tribute* March 1996: 10.

_____. "Parties Claim It's a Cover-up." *City Press* 3 March 1996: 1.

_____. "*Sarafina O*." *Daily Dispatch* 8 March 1996: 14.

_____. "AIDS Message 'Not Effective.'" *Cape Times* 11 March 1996: 1.

_____. "*Sarafina* Shocker." *Saturday Paper* 30 March 1996: 1.

_____. "*Sarafina* 2—Next: The Video?" *Eastern Province Herald* 4 June 1996: 4.

_____. "Rise in HIV-positive Cases." *Natal Witness* 30 July 1996: 4.

Arewa, E.O. "A Classification of the Folktales of the Northern East African Cattle Area by Type." Ph.D. dissertation, University of California, Berkeley, 1966.

Armah, Ai Kwei. "The Romantic Response to the Industrial Revolution: A Sociological Study of the Works of William Blake (1757-1827) and William Wordsworth (1770-1850)." Unpublished B.A. thesis, Harvard University, 1963.

Armah, Aryeequaye. "The Offal Kind." *Drum* (January 1964): 35-39; rpt. in *Harper's Magazine* 1424 (January 1969): 79-84.

Armah, Aryee Quaye. "Pan-Africanism and the White Man's Burden." *Harvard Journal of Negro Affairs* 1, 2 (1965): 27-40.

Armah, Ayi Kwei. *The Beautyful Ones Are Not Yet Born*. Boston: Houghton Mifflin, 1968.

_____. *Fragments*. Boston: Houghton Mifflin, 1970.

_____. *Why Are We So Blest?* New York: Doubleday, 1972.

_____. *Two Thousand Seasons*. Nairobi: East African Publishing House, 1973.

_____. "Larsony, or Fiction as Criticism of Fiction." *Asemka* 4 (1976): 1-14.

_____. *The Healers*. Nairobi: East African Publishing House, 1978.

_____. "One Writer's Education." *West Africa* 26 August 1985: 1752-53.

_____. *Osiris Rising*. Popenguine, Senegal: Per Ankh, 1995.

Armah, G. "Ghana." *The Grotonian* (November 1959): 11-15.

_____. "East, West, or Neuter?" *The Grotonian* (February 1960): 71-75.

_____. "Cold Thaw—Deep Freeze." *The Grotonian* (May 1960): 130-31.

Armah, George A. K. "The Ball." *Harvard Advocate* 98, 2 (1964): 35-40.

Bâ, Sylvia Washington. *The Concept of Negritude in the Poetry of Léopold Sédar Senghor*. Princeton, NJ: Princeton University Press, 1973.

Bamgbose, Ayo. *The Novels of D.O. Fagunwa*. Benin City: Ethiope Publishing Corp., 1974.

Bascom, William. "Folklore Research in Africa." *Journal of American Folklore* 77 (1964): 12-31.

Belvaude, Catherine E. *Amos Tutuola et l'univers du conte africain*. Paris: L'Harmattan, 1989.

Bentsi-Enchill, Nii K. and Kojo. "For an Afro-African Literature." *West Africa* 22-29 December 1980: 2604-05.

Berman, Kathy. "Ngema and SA's Musical Mousetrap." *Weekly Mail* 16-23 April 1992: 32.

Beti, Mongo. *Mission to Kala*. London: Frederick Muller, 1958.

Bruin, John [pseud. for Dennis Brutus]. *Thoughts Abroad*. Del Valle, TX: Troubadour Press, 1975.

Brutus, Dennis. *A Simple Lust*. London: Heinemann, 1973.

Carter, Chiara "Comedy of Bungles." *City Press* 9 June 1966: 4.

Chisholm, Fiona. "Reviewers' Thumbs-down for Zuma Play." *Cape Times* 11 March 1996: 1, 3.

Clarke, Kenneth W. "Motif-Index of the Folktales of Culture Area V, West Africa." Ph.D. dissertation, Indiana University, 1958.

Clarke, Peter. "The Notice on the Wall." *Mundus Artium* 9, 2 (1976): 49.

Coan, Stephen. "*Sarafina*: There's Never Been a Theatrical Budget Like It." *Natal Witness* 5 March 1996: 9.

Coleman, Carl. "No Grammy Shock for Ngema." *Daily News* 9 March 1995. 1

Collins, Harold R. *Amos Tutuola*. New York: Twayne, 1969.

Cull, Patrick. "*Sarafina 2* Terminated by SA Government." *Eastern Province Herald* 6 June 1996: 2.

Davis, Gaye. "Star Players in the Financial Flop." *Mail and Guardian* 7-13 June 1996: 4-5.

du Bois, Duncan. "Distorted AIDS Factor." *Natal Witness* 9 July 1996: 10.

Emenyonu, Ernest. "Early Fiction in Igbo." *Research in African Literatures* 4, 1 (1973): 7-20.

Ensor, Robert. *The Novels of Peter Abrahams and the Rise of Nationalism in Africa*. Essen, Germany: Die Blaue Eule, 1992.

Ezugu, Michael Amadihe. "The Influence of Theme on Technique in the Novels of Ayi Kwei Armah." Unpublished M.A. thesis, University of Nigeria, Nsukka, 1981.

Frederikse, Julie. *The Unbreakable Thread: Non-racialism in South Africa*. Johannesburg: Ravan Press, 1990.

Gacheru, Margaretta wa. "Ngugi wa Thiong'o Still Bitter Over His Detention." *Weekly Review* 5 January 1979: 30-32.

Gérard, Albert S. *Four African Literatures: Xhosa, Sotho, Zulu, Amharic*. Berkeley and Los Angeles: University of California Press, 1971.

Gevisser, Mark. "'I Should Be Paid a Million Rands.'" *Mail and Guardian* 8-14 March 1996: 1, 16.

_____. "Sarafina of the Health System." *Mail and Guardian* 22-28 March 1996: 14.

Harries, Lyndon. "Swahili Literature in the National Context." *Review of National Literatures*. 2, 2 (1971): 38-65.

Isaacson, Maureen. "A Musical Magician Comes to the Playhouse." *Sunday Star* 9 January 1994: 2.

Jahn, Janheinz. *A History of Neo-African Literature: Writing in Two Continents*. London: Faber and Faber, 1966.

_____. "Modern African Literature: Bibliographical Spectrum." *Review of National Literatures* 2, 2 (1971): 224-42.

_____, and Claus Peter Dressler. *Bibliography of Creative African Writing*. Nendeln: Kraus, 1971.

Jones, Eldred. "*The Palm-Wine Drinkard*—Fourteen Years On." *Bulletin of the Association for African Literature in English* 4 (1966): 24-30.

Jones, Laura. *Nothing Except Ourselves: The Harsh Times and Bold Theater of South Africa's Mbongeni Ngema*. New York: Penguin, 1994.

Khumalo, Reginald. "Sloppy Show Disappoints." *Natal Witness* 11 January 1996: 7.

Klipple, May A. "African Folktales with Foreign Analogues." Ph.D. dissertation, Indiana University, 1938.

Kunene, Daniel P. *The Works of Thomas Mofolo: Summaries and Critiques*. Los Angeles: African Studies Center, University of California at Los Angeles, 1967.

Lambrecht, Winifred. "A Tale Type Index for Central Africa." Ph.D. dissertation, University of California, Berkeley, 1967.

Laye, Camara. *Le Regard du roi*. Paris: Plon, 1954.

Lee, Peta. "The Only Ngema in Town." *Sunday Times Magazine* 26 February 1995: 34.

Lindfors, Bernth. "Amos Tutuola's *The Palm-Wine Drinkard* and Oral Tradition." *Critique* 11 (1968-69): 42-50.

_____. "The African Politician's Changing Image in African Literature in English." *Journal of the Developing Areas* 4 (1969): 13-28.

_____. "Oral Tradition and the Individual Literary Talent." *Studies in the Novel* 4 (1972): 200-17.

_____. "Ayi Kwei Armah's Achimota Writings." *Commonwealth: Essays and Studies* 18, 1 (1995): 62-72.

_____. "Dennis Brutus, Texas Poet." *Critical Perspectives on Dennis Brutus*. Colorado Springs: Three Continents Press, 1995. 162-72.

_____, Ian Munro, Richard Priebe and Reinhard Sander, eds. *Palaver: Interviews with Five African Writers in Texas*. Austin: African and Afro-American Research Institute, University of Texas at Austin, 1972.

_____, and Reinhard Sander, eds. *Twentieth-Century Caribbean and Black African Writers*. Dictionary of Literary Biography, Vol. 117. Detroit: Gale Research, 1992.

Lund, Troye. "*Sarafina 2* Video Goes On Despite Row." *Star* 5 June 1996: 1-2.

MacLiam, Garalt. "It's Rock, Roll and Bop as *Sarafina 2* Celebrates People Power in Soweto." *Star* 11 March 1996.

_____. "It's Better Than a Poke in the Eye with a Sharp Stick." *Star* 13 March 1996: 7-8.

Maes-Jelinek, Hena, Gordon Collier, and Geoffrey V. Davis, eds. *A Talent(ed) Digger: Creations, Cameos and Essays in Honour of Anna Rutherford*. Amsterdam and Atlanta: Rodopi, 1996.

Makgabutlane, Sol. "Into *the* Mainstream." *Tribute* April 1990: 20-24.

_____. "*Sarafina!* Five Years of Success." *Tribute* February 1992: 38-40.

Makoe, Abbey. "*Sarafina* Not a Total Sham, But Waste of R14-m." *Argus* 11 March 1996: 3.

Matthews, James, and Gladys Thomas. *Cry Rage!* Johannesburg: Spro-cas Publications, 1972.

Matthews, James, ed. *Black Voices Shout!* Athlone: Blac
	Publishing House, 1974.

Mbelolo ya Mpiku, "Introduction à la littérature kikongo."
	Research in African Literatures 3, 2 (1972): 122-30.

Mendel, Delores. "Mbongeni Ngema." *Club* April 1990: 18-19.

Metsoamere, Victor. "Ngema Does it by Ear." *Suwetan* 10
	February 1995: 8.

Modisane, Bloke. "Short Story Writing in Black South Africa."
	American Society of African Culture Newsletter 5, 8
	(1963): 2-3.

Mondear, Joseph. "'Slight and Trivial Message' Woven into
	Sarafina 2 Production." *Star* 26 March 1996: 16.

Mphahlele, Ezekiel. *The African Image.* London: Faber, 1962.

_____. "A Reply." *African Literature and the Universities.*
	Ed. Gerald Moore. Ibadan: Ibadan University
	Press for the Congress of Cultural Freedom,
	1965.

Mtshali, Oswald Joseph. *Sounds of a Cowhide Drum.*
	Johannesburg: Renoster Books, 1971.

Munene, Fibi. "The Last Word." *Daily Nation* 14 December
	1977: 19.

Mungai wa Kamau. "Ngugi Play Banned Because
	'Provocative.'" *Nairobi Times* 4 December 1977:
	1.

Ngema, Mbongeni. *The Best of Mbongeni Ngema.* Braamfontein:
	Skotaville Publishers, 1995.

Ngema, Vusi. "Musical Which Tackles AIDS But Desperately
	Seeks a Story." *Natal Witness* 6 January 1996: 7.

Ngidi, Thami. "'The Show Will Go On.'" *Saturday Paper* 9 March 1996: 4.

Ngugi wa Thiong'o. *A Grain of Wheat*. London: Heinemann, 1967.

_____. *Homecoming: Essays on African and Caribbean Literature, Culture and Politics*. New York: Lawrence Hill, 1972.

_____. *Petals of Blood*. London: Heinemann, 1977.

_____. *Caitaani Mutharaba-ini*. Nairobi: Heinemann, 1980. Translated as *Devil on the Cross*. London: Heinemann, 1982.

_____, and Ngugi wa Mirii. *Ngaahika Ndeenda*. Nairobi: Heinemann, 1982. Translated as *I Will Marry When I Want*. London and Exeter, NH: Heinemann, 1982.

Nkosi, Lewis. "African Fiction: Part One, South Africa: Protest." *Africa Report* 7, 9 (1962): 3-6.

_____. "Conversation with Chinua Achebe." *Africa Report* 9, 7 (1964): 19-21.

Noble, Lawrence M. Letter and memo to Reverend John Crocker, 20 August 1958.

Nyatsumba, Kaizer. "They Take the Cake." *Argus* 13 March 1996: 18; rpt. as "The Truth Will Soon Out." *Daily News* 14 March 1996: 16.

Obiechina, Emmanuel. "Amos Tutuola and Oral Tradition." *Présence Africaine* 65 (1968): 85-106.

Ogungbesan, Kolawole. *The Writings of Peter Abrahams*. New York: Africana Publishing Co., 1979.

Okafor, Clem Abiaziem. "The Inscrutability of the Gods: Motivation of Behavior in Chinua Achebe's *Arrow of God.*" *Présence Africaine* 63 (1967): 207-14.

Osinya, Alumidi. *The Amazing Saga of Field Marshal Abdulla Sulim Fisi, or How the Hyena Got His.* Nairobi: Joe Publications and Transafrica Book Distributors, 1977.

Palmer, Mabel. *The History of the Indians in Natal.* London: Oxford University Press, 1957; rpt. Westport CT: Greenwood Press, 1977.

p'Bitek, Okot. *Song of Lawino: A Lament.* Nairobi: East African Publishing House, 1966.

_____. *Song of Ocol.* Nairobi: East African Publishing House, 1970.

_____. *Two Songs: Song of Prisoner; Song of Malaya.* Nairobi: East African Publishing House, 1971.

_____. *Africa's Cultural Revolution.* Nairobi: Macmillan Books for Africa, 1973.

Pifer, Alan. Letter to Bernth Lindfors, 10 September 1995.

Ramklown, Annesh. "Ngema's Latest *Sarafina* a Dismal Failure." *Natal Witness Echo* 11 January 1996: 5.

Rice, John Alden. "Council Votes Not to Recommend 'African and Afro-American' Club." *The Harvard Crimson* 7 May 1963: 1-2.

Robbins, David. "Experts Slam AIDS Play." *Star* 11 March 1966: 1.

Saro-Wiwa, Ken. *Sozaboy.* Port Harcourt and Epsom, England: Saros International, 1985.

_____. "Nigerian Literature is Alive and Well." *ANA Review* 7, 9 (1992): 1, 16-17.

Sartre, Jean-Paul. *Black Orpheus*. Trans. S.W. Allen. Paris: Présence Africaine, 1963.

_____. *Basi and Company: A Modern African Folktale*. Port Harcourt and Epsom, England: Saros International, 1987.

_____. *Basi and Company: Four Television Plays*. Port Harcourt and Epsom, England: Saros International, 1988.

Scott, John. "*Sarafina 2*'s New Wisecracking Star." *Cape Times* 13 March 1996: 16.

Senghor, Léopold Sédar. *Léopold Sédar Senghor: Prose and Poetry*. Ed. and trans. John Reed and Clive Wake. London: Oxford University Press, 1963.

Serote, Mongane Wally. *Yakhal'inkomo*. Johannesburg: Renoster, 1972.

Serumaga, Robert. "Chinua Achebe Interviewed by Robert Serumaga." *Cultural Events in Africa* 28 (1967): i-iv supp.

Sherriffs, Pamela. "AIDS: It's Too Costly to Play Around." *Natal Witness* 1 March 1966: 15.

Sherwood, Adrian. Letter to James Gibbs, 3 July 1995.

Sidley, Pat. "AIDS Spreads as Money Lies Idle." *Sunday Times* 9 June 1996: 4.

Simon, Janine. "Puppet Players Query *Sarafina* Costs." *Star* 1 March 1996: 1-2.

Singh, Ansuyah R. *Behold the Earth Mourns*. Cape Town: N.p., n.d.

Skinner, Neil. "Realism and Fantasy in Hausa Literature." *Review of National Literatures* 2, 2 (1971): 167-87.

Soyinka, Wole. "The Writer in an African State." *Transition* 31 (1967): 11-13.

Spratt, Betsy. "The Kids Liked It But Did It Teach Them Anything About AIDS?" *Sunday Independent* 10 March 1996: 1.

Stuart, Sapa and Brian. "Call for *Sarafina II* Probe." *Citizen* 29 February 1996: 1-2.

Thompson, Stith. *Motif-Index of Folk-Literature.* Bloomington: Indiana University Press, 1955-58.

Tivoneleni Vavasati AIDS Awareness Project. "Ministry's Musical Should Sing a New Song." *Mail and Guardian* 23-29 February 1996: 28.

Vanderhaeghen, Yves. "The Play that Shamed the ANC." *Natal Witness* 11 July 1996: 6.

van der Walt, Terry, and Sam Sole. "Ngema's Tender Touch." *Sunday Tribune* 11 February 1996: 1, 5.

Wade, Michael. *Peter Abrahams.* London: Evans, 1972.

Wellek, René, and Austin Warren. *Theory of Literature.* New York: Harcourt, Brace, 1949.

Wright, Derek. *Ayi Kwei Armah's Africa: The Sources of His Fiction.* London: Hans Zell, 1989.

Index